Fostering Now

LAW, REGULATIONS, GUIDANCE AND STANDARDS (ENGLAND)

**Fergus Smith and Chris Brann
with Alexandra Conroy Harris**

CoramBAAF Adoption and Fostering Academy
41 Brunswick Square
London WC1N 1AZ
www.corambaaf.org.uk

Coram Academy Limited, registered as a company limited by guarantee in England and Wales number 9697712, part of the Coram group, charity number 312278

© Fergus Smith and Chris Brann, 2016
Reprinted 2020 with minor revisions

British Library Cataloguing in Publication Data
A catalogue record for this book is available from the British Library

ISBN 978 1 910039 46 5

Designed and typeset by Helen Joubert Design
Printed in the UK by The Lavenham Press

All rights reserved. Except as permitted under the Copyright, Designs and Patents Act 1988, this publication may not be reproduced, stored in a retrieval system, or transmitted in any form or by any means, without the prior written permission of the publisher.

No part of this publication may be reproduced without the written consent of the author.

Contents

Introduction	1
Definitions (in alphabetical order)	3
Routes into Foster Care	8
Local Authority General Duties towards Looked After Children [ss.22, 23, 24 & Sch.2 CA 1989 as amended]	9

Care Planning, Placement & Case Review (England) Regulations 2010 (as amended) — 19

Interpretations & Application of CPP & CR (England) Regulations 2010 (as amended)	20
Arrangements for Looking After a Child	22
Placements: General Provisions	29
Provision for Different Types of Placement: Placement of a Child in Care with Parents etc	40
Provision for Different Types of Placement: Placement with Local Authority Foster Parents	44
Provision for Different Types of Placement: Other Arrangements	51
Visits by Responsible Authority's Representative etc	52
Reviews of the Child's Case	55
Arrangements to be made when the Responsible Authority is Considering Ceasing to Look After a Child [Regs.39–44]	60
Independent Reviewing Officers & Independent Visitors [Regs.45–47]	65
Miscellaneous [Regs.48–51]	67

Fostering Services (England) Regulations 2011 (as amended) — 71

Statement of Purpose & Children's Guide [Regs.1–4]	72
Management of Fostering Service [Regs.5–10]	73
Conduct of Fostering Service [Regs.11–22 Fostering Services (England) Regulations 2011]	77
Approval of Foster Parents [Regs.23–32 Fostering Services (England) Regulations 2011]	86
Fostering Agencies: Miscellaneous [Regs.33–41 Fostering Services (England) Regulations 2011]	106

National Minimum Standards (NMS) — 115
Values/Principles — 116
Legal Status of the National Minimum Standards — 117
Structure & Approach to Inspection — 118

Child-Focused Standards — 121
Standard 1 – Child's Wishes & Feelings & Views of Those Significant to Her/Him — 122
Standard 2 – Promoting a Positive Identity, Potential & Valuing Diversity through Individualised Care — 123
Standard 3 – Promoting Positive Behaviour & Relationships — 124
Standard 4 – Protecting from Abuse & Neglect — 126
Standard 5 – Children Missing from Care — 127
Standard 6 – Promoting Good Health & Wellbeing — 129
Standard 7 – Leisure Activities — 131
Standard 8 – Promoting Educational Achievement — 132
Standard 9 – Promoting & Supporting Contact — 133
Standard 10 – Providing a Suitable Physical Environment for the Foster Child — 135
Standard 11 – Preparation for a Placement — 136
Standard 12 – Promoting Independence & Moves to Adulthood & Leaving Care — 138

Standards of Fostering Service — 141
Standard 13 – Recruiting and Assessing Foster Carers who can Meet the Needs of Looked After Children — 142
Standard 14 – Fostering Panels & Fostering Service's Decision-Maker — 144
Standard 15 – Matching the Child with a Placement that Meets their Assessed Needs — 145
Standard 16 – Statement of Purpose & Children's Guide — 147
Standard 17 – Fitness to Provide or Manage the Administration of a Fostering Service — 148
Standard 18 – Financial Viability & Changes Affecting Business Continuity — 150
Standard 19 – Suitability to Work with Children — 151
Standard 20 – Learning & Development of Foster Carers — 153
Standard 21 – Supervision & Support of Foster Carers — 155

Standard 22 – Handling Allegations & Suspicions of Harm	157
Standard 23 – Learning, Development & Qualification of Staff	160
Standard 24 – Staff Support & Supervision	162
Standard 25 – Managing Effectively & Efficiently & Monitoring the Service	163
Standard 26 – Records	166
Standard 27 – Fitness of Premises for use as a Fostering Service	167
Standard 28 – Payment to Carers	168
Standard 29 – Notification of Significant Events	170
Standard 30 – Family & Friends as Foster Carers	171
Standard 31 – Placement Plan & Review	173
Fees & Frequency of Inspections	**175**
Registration Fees [The Her Majesty's Chief Inspector of Education, Children's Services & Skills (Fees & Frequency of Inspections) (Children's Homes etc) Regulations 2015]	176
Appendix 1: Source Documents	177
Appendix 2: Foster Carers' Charter	179
Further Reading	181

Abbreviations

CA 1989 = Children Act 1989

CAFA 2014 = Children and Families Act 2014

Cafcass = Children & Families Courts Advisory & Support Service

CPP & CR Regulations = Care Planning, Placement and Case Review (England) Regulations 2010

CSA 2000 = Care Standards Act 2000

CYPA 2008 = Children & Young Persons Act 2008

ISA = Independent Safeguarding Authority

PA 1997 = Police Act 1997

POCA 1999 = Protection of Children Act 1999

SVGA 2006 = Safeguarding Vulnerable Groups Act 2006

CSWA 2017 = Children and Social Work Act 2017

Notes about the authors

Fergus Smith is the director of Children Act Enterprises Ltd (www.caeuk.org), an independent social work consultancy that has published over 20 "personal guides" to family and criminal law, undertaken several commissioned research projects and provided other consultancy and training to numerous local authorities. For the last 15 years, Fergus has specialised in conducting serious case reviews.

Chris Brann has recently retired after 35 years in children's social work. Chris has extensive practice and management experience of fostering, adoption and planning for looked after children.

From 2008–2018, Fergus, Chris and their colleague Laura Ritchie operated Services for Children (SfC), an independent fostering agency twice evaluated as "outstanding" by the regulator, Ofsted.

Alexandra Conroy Harris is CoramBAAF's Legal Consultant. She is a barrister with over twenty years' experience of representing parents, children and local authorities in care and adoption proceedings. She spent nine years as a senior social services lawyer for a London borough, during which she was a committed user of this guide's previous edition. She has worked for CoramBAAF and BAAF since 2008 and produces the Legal Notes for the *Adoption & Fostering* journal.

Introduction

- This revised guide is for use in England, by those who provide, or work in fostering services and agencies (managers, practitioners and foster carers) as well as by those social workers who make and support placements.

- It is intended to facilitate understanding of the obligations and expectations of all relevant law, regulations, statutory and non-statutory guidance. Appendix 2 reproduces the 2011 'Foster Carers' Charter' issued by the Secretary of State which sets out basic standards and principles for carers and their children, and the expectations of how councils should support foster families.

- The Chief Inspector of the Office for Standards in Children's Services, Education and Skills (Ofsted) assesses, based on the Fostering Services (England) Regulations 2011 as amended (compliance with which is mandatory), and achievement of the national minimum standards (issued by the Secretary of State under s.23(1) CSA 2000), whether services provided by a local authority, independent fostering agency (IFA) or a voluntary organisation are satisfactory.

- When the Chief Inspector makes any decision about registration, cancellation, variation or imposition of conditions, s/he must take the national minimum standards and any other factors considered reasonable and relevant into account.

- With respect to IFAs and voluntary organisations, if a regulation is breached and an offence committed, providers will be given a notice setting out:
    - Regulation breached
    - How the service is considered deficient
    - What must be done to remedy the deficiency
    - A timescale for the deficiency to be remedied.

- If the deficiency is not remedied, a prosecution may follow.

Introduction

- In the case of a local authority service, the enforcement route is via the Secretary of State to whom the Chief Inspector will report a substantial failure to meet a regulation. If there is a failure which is not substantial, the Chief Inspector may serve an enforcement notice under s.47(5) CSA 2000.

Definitions (in alphabetical order)

Child

- A person aged less than 18 years old.

Distant Placement

- A 'distant placement' is defined as one which is outside the area of the responsible authority and not within the area of any adjoining local authority (distant placements must be approved by the responsible authority's director of children's services (DCS)) [reg.11(5) CPP&CR Regs.2010 as amended by the Children's Homes and Looked After Children (Miscellaneous Amendments) (England) Regulations 2013].

Eligible Child

- An eligible child is a looked after child aged 16 or 17 who has been looked after for a total of at least 13 weeks which began after s/he reached 14 and ends after s/he reaches 16 [para.19B Sch.2 CA 1989 and reg.40 CPP&CR Regs.2010].

Former Relevant Child

- A former relevant child is a young person aged 18 or over who was either an eligible or a relevant child (the local authority has duties in relation to this group until they reach 21 or 25 in the case of those who are pursuing a programme of education or training) [s.23C CA 1989].

Foster Parent [Reg.2 Fostering Services (England) Regulations 2011 as amended by reg.6 Care Planning, Placement and Case Review and Fostering Services (Miscellaneous Amendments) Regulations 2013]

- A foster parent is a person who is approved under the Fostering Services Regulations and (except in reg.25–30 Care Planning Regulations) includes a person with whom a child is placed under reg.24 of the Care

Definitions (in alphabetical order)

Planning Regulations (temporary approval of a relative, friend or other connected person).

Fostering Service [Reg.2 Fostering Services (England) Regulations 2011]

- A fostering service means:
  - A fostering agency as defined in s.4(4) CSA 2000, i.e. a private or voluntary organisation that carries out fostering functions of a local authority or
  - A local authority fostering service.
- An 'independent fostering agency' is one falling within the definition of s.4(4)(a) CSA 2000, i.e. discharging functions of local authorities in connection with placing of children with foster parents.

Fostering Service Provider

- A fostering service provider means:
  - In relation to a fostering agency, a registered person
  - In relation to a local authority fostering service, a local authority.

Independent Reviewing Officer (IRO)

- An IRO means the independent reviewing officer appointed for a child under s.25A(1) CA 1989.

Long Term Foster Placement

- A long term foster placement means an arrangement made by the responsible authority for C to be placed with F where:
  - C's plan for permanence (the long term plan for C's upbringing) is foster care
  - F has agreed to act as C's foster carer until C ceases to be looked after and
  - The responsible authority has confirmed the nature of the arrangements to F, P and C.

Definitions (in alphabetical order)

- Any reference to the responsible authority placing C in such a placement if C is already there, includes leaving her/him in a long term placement [reg.2(1) CPP&CR Regulations 2010 as inserted by reg.3 Care Planning and Fostering (Miscellaneous Amendments) (England) Regulations 2015].

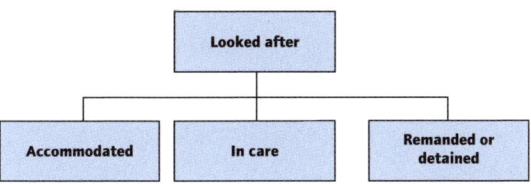

Looked After [s.22 CA 1989]

- A child who is 'looked after' by a local authority may be 'accommodated', 'in care' or 'remanded/detained'.
- Accommodation is a voluntary arrangement. The local authority does not gain parental responsibility and no notice is required for removal of the child.
- In care means that a court has made a child subject of a Care Order which gives the local authority parental responsibility and (some) authority to limit the parents' exercise of their continuing parental responsibility.
- The local authority has specific authority to detain those who fall into the third category who may do so because of:
  - Remand by a court following criminal charges
  - Detention following arrest by police
  - An Emergency Protection Order or Child Assessment Order
  - A 'criminal' Supervision Order with a residence requirement.

NB. With the exception of Emergency Protection Orders, the local authority does not gain parental responsibility when detaining a child.

Definitions (in alphabetical order)

Parent [Reg.2(1) Fostering Services (England) Regulations 2011]

- A parent, in relation to a child, includes any person who has parental responsibility for her/him.

Parent & Child Arrangements

- The interpretation of this term is provided in reg.2 of the Fostering Services (England) Regulations 2011 as 'arrangements made by a local authority for a parent and their child to live with a foster parent, whether or not the parent or child is placed with the foster parent'.

Placing Authority

- 'Placing authority' in relation to a child means the local authority or voluntary organisation (as the case may be) responsible for the child's placement.

Registered Manager [Reg.2(1) Fostering Services (England) Regulations 2011]

- The registered manager means the person who is registered under Part 2 CSA 2000 as the manager of that agency.

Registered Person [Reg.2(1) Fostering Services (England) Regulations 2011]

- The registered person means any person who is the registered provider or the registered manager of a fostering agency.

Registered Provider [Reg.2(1) Fostering Services (England) Regulations 2011]

- The registered provider means the person who is registered under Part 2 of the CSA 2000 as the person carrying on a fostering agency.

  NB. In the case of a voluntary organisation which places children with foster parents under s.59(1) CA 1989, s.121(4) CSA 2000 defines the 'person carrying on a fostering agency' as the voluntary organisation itself.

Definitions (in alphabetical order)

Relevant Child

- A relevant child is a young person aged 16 or 17 who was an 'eligible child' but is no longer looked after [s.23A CA 1989 and reg.4 Children (Leaving Care) (England) Regulations 2001].

Responsible Authority [Reg.2 Fostering Services (England) Regulations 2011]

- The responsible authority in relation to a child is the local authority that looks after her/him.

'Staying Put' [s.23CZA CA 1989 as introduced by s.98 CAFA 2014]

- An arrangement under which a 'former relevant child' and a former foster parent of that person immediately before s/he ceased to be looked after by the local authority continue to live together after the child has ceased to be looked after.

- It is the duty of the local authority to monitor the staying put arrangement and (until s/he reaches the age of 21) provide advice, assistance and support (which must include financial support as per s.23CZA(4) CA 1989) to the former relevant child and former foster parent with a view to maintaining the staying put arrangement.

- The duty to support does *not* apply if the local authority considers that such an arrangement is not consistent with the welfare of the former relevant child.

NB. When carrying out an assessment of the needs of an 'eligible child' placed with a foster parent, the local authority must determine whether facilitating a staying put arrangement would be appropriate. If it is adjudged to be appropriate and the eligible child and foster parents wish that arrangement the local authority is obliged to make it [Sch.2 para.19BA CA 1989].

Routes into Foster Care

Accommodating a Child [s.20 CA 1989]

- One of the family support services the local authority must provide is that of 'accommodating' (in family or residential settings) anyone under 18 'in need' who requires it as a result of:
  - There being no person with parental responsibility for her/him
  - S/he being lost or having been abandoned or
  - The person who has been caring for her/him being prevented temporarily or permanently (for whatever reason) from providing suitable care/accommodation.
- This service is a completely voluntary arrangement and the local authority does not gain parental responsibility.
- A person with parental responsibility has the right to remove a child from such an arrangement [s.20(8) CA 1989] but:
  - A person named in a Child Arrangements Order as a person with whom the child shall live, or a holder of a Special Guardianship Order or a person who has care of the child under wardship, can override parental wishes [s.20(9) CA 1989 as amended by Sch.3 para. 59 ACA 2002 and s.12 and Sch.2 CAF 2014].
  - A young person of 16 or 17 could overrule her/his parent's wishes to remove them [s.20(11) CA 1989].
- Anyone who does not have parental responsibility for a child but does have actual care of her/him may do what is reasonable in the circumstances to safeguard and promote the child's welfare [s.3(5) CA 1989].
- If 'significant harm' seems likely, emergency protection measures could be used.
- A local authority may accommodate a child in their area if they consider that it would safeguard their welfare [s.20(4) CA 1989].

Local Authority General Duties towards Looked After Children

Accommodating a 16- or 17-Year-Old [s.20(3) CA 1989]

- A local authority must provide accommodation to a young person in the above age group if s/he is 'in need' and her/his welfare would otherwise be 'seriously prejudiced'.

Accommodating a Young Person Aged 16–20 Years Old [s.20(5) CA 1989]

- A local authority may provide accommodation in any Community Home which accepts 16+ year olds if it considers it would safeguard or promote the young person's welfare.

Other Obligations to Accommodate [s.21(1), (2) CA 1989]

- When asked, the local authority must 'accommodate' those:
  - Removed from home on an Emergency Protection Order, Child Assessment Order or an Interim Care Order
  - In police protection
  - Remanded by a court
  - Detained under the Police & Criminal Evidence Act 1984
  - On a Supervision Order with residence requirements (Children & Young Persons Act 1969 [s.12AA].

Local Authority General Duties towards Looked After Children [ss.22, 23, 24 & Sch.2 CA 1989 as amended]

Duties: All Children

- Safeguard and promote welfare and make reasonable efforts to allow the child access to ordinary services as though still at home.
- Particular duty to promote the child's educational welfare [s.22(3A) CA 1989].

Local Authority General Duties towards Looked After Children

- Endeavour, unless not reasonably practical or consistent with welfare, to promote contact between the child and:
  - Parents, and others with parental responsibility
  - Relatives, friends or persons connected with her/him.
- Take reasonable steps to keep parents and those with parental responsibility informed of the child's location.
- Before making any decision, ascertain the wishes/feelings of:
  - The child
  - The parent/s and any others who have parental responsibility and relevant others.
- Give due consideration to these views (having regard in the case of the child to level of understanding) religion, racial origin, cultural and linguistic background.

  NB. A local authority may act in a manner that is contrary to the above in order to protect the public from serious injury.

- So far as is practical and consistent with welfare, place the child with:
  - Parents
  - Someone who has parental responsibility
  - (For a child in care), any previous Residence Order holder (a person named in a Child Arrangements Order as a person with whom the child shall live)
  - Relatives or friends or
  - Other person connected with her/him.
- If a child has to be placed with strangers, ensure the placement is near home and with any siblings.
- Prepare the child for leaving looked after status.
- The local authority must also take reasonable steps to:
  - Reduce criminal/civil proceedings which might lead to Care or Supervision Orders
  - Avoid the use of secure accommodation

Local Authority General Duties towards Looked After Children

- Encourage children not to commit crime.

Provision of Accommodation & Maintenance for Looked After Children

- By virtue of s.8(1) C&YPA 2008, s.23 CA 1989 is substituted as follows by:

  - *Provision of accommodation for children in care:* when a child is in the care of a local authority, it is its duty to provide her/him with accommodation [s.22A CA 1989].
  - *Maintenance of looked after children:* it is the duty of a local authority to maintain a child it is looking after in other respects apart from the provision of accommodation [s.22B CA 1989].

- S.22C *(ways in which looked after children are to be accommodated and maintained)* applies as follows when a local authority is looking after a child C [s.22C(1) CA 1989].

- The local authority must make arrangements for C to live with a person who falls within s.22C(3) (but subject to s.22C(4)) [s.22C(2) CA 1989].

- A person (P) falls within subsection 22C(3) if:

  - P is a parent of C
  - P is *not* a parent of C but has parental responsibility for her/him; or
  - In a case when C is in the care of the local authority and there was a Child Arrangements Order in force with respect of her/him immediately before the care order was made, P was a person named in the order as a person with whom the child was to live [s.22C(3) CA 1989].

  NB. S.22C(2) does not require the local authority to make arrangements of the kind mentioned in that subsection if doing so would not be consistent with C's welfare or would not be reasonably practicable [s.22C(4) CA 1989].

- If the local authority is unable to make arrangements under s.22C(2), it must place C in the placement which is, in its opinion, the most appropriate placement available [s.22C(5) CA 1989].

- In s.22C(5) 'placement' means placement:
    - With an individual who is a relative, friend or other person connected with C and who is also a local authority foster parent
    - With a local authority foster parent who does not fall within the above category
    - In a children's home in respect of which a person is registered under Part 2 Care Standards Act 2000; or
    - (Subject to s.22D), placement in accordance with other arrangements which comply with any regulations made for the purposes of s.22 [s.22C(6) CA 1989].

- In determining the most appropriate placement for C, the local authority must, subject to other provisions of this Part (in particular, duties under s.22 CA 1989):
    - Give preference to a placement falling within the first paragraph in s.22C(6) above other placements falling within the other three paragraphs of that section
    - Comply, so far as is reasonably practicable in all the circumstances of C's case, with the requirements of s.22C(8) and
    - Comply with s.22C(9) unless that is not reasonably practicable [s.22C(7) CA 1989].

- The local authority must ensure the placement is such that:
    - It allows C to live near C's home
    - It does not disrupt C's education or training
    - If C has a sibling for whom the local authority is also providing accommodation, it enables C and the sibling to live together
    - If C is disabled, the accommodation provided is suitable to C's particular needs [s.22C(8) CA 1989].

- The placement must be such that C is provided with accommodation within the local authority's area [s.22C(9) CA 1989].

- Where a local authority is considering adoption for a child, ss.(7)–(9) do not apply and the LA must consider placing the child with a foster parent who has been approved as an adopter.

Local Authority General Duties towards Looked After Children

- The local authority may determine the terms:
  - Of any arrangements it makes under s.22C(2) in relation to C (including terms as to payment); and
  - On which it places C with a local authority foster parent (including terms as to payment but subject to any order made under s.49 Children Act 2004) [s.22C(10) CA 1989].

  NB. The appropriate national authority may make regulations for, and in connection with, the purposes of s.22 [s.22C(11) CA 1989].

- 22D (review of child's case before making alternative arrangements for accommodation) provides that:
  - When a local authority is providing accommodation for a child (C) other than by arrangements under s.22C(6)(d), it must not make such arrangements for her/him unless it has decided to do so in consequence of a review of C's case carried out in accordance with regulations made under s.26 CA 1989.

  NB. s.22D(1) does not prevent a local authority making arrangements for C under s.22C(6)(d), if it is satisfied that in order to safeguard her/his welfare it is necessary to make such arrangements and to do so as a matter of urgency [s.22D(2).

- 22E (children's homes provided by appropriate national authority) provides that:
  - When a local authority places a child it is looking after in a children's home provided, equipped and maintained by an appropriate national authority under s.82(5), it must do so on such terms as that national authority may from time to time determine.

- 22F (regulations as to children looked after by local authorities) provides that Part 2 of Schedule 2 has effect for the purposes of making further provision as to children looked after by local authorities and in particular as to the regulations which may be made under s.22C(11).

- Schedule 1 (which makes amendments supplementary to, and consequential on, the provisions of s.22 including a power to make

Local Authority General Duties towards Looked After Children

regulations about an 'independent review mechanism' for certain decisions in relation to foster parents) has effect [s.8(2)].

Ensuring Visits to Looked After Children & Others

- S.15 CYPA 2008 introduced a s.23ZA to the CA 1989 which applies to a:
  - Child looked after by a local authority
  - Child or young person who was looked after but who has ceased to be looked after by it as a result of prescribed circumstances [s.23ZA(1)].

- It is the duty of the local authority to:
  - Ensure that a person to whom s.23 applies is visited by a 'representative' of the authority
  - Arrange for appropriate advice, support and assistance to be available to a person to whom s.23 applies who seeks it from that local authority [s.23ZA(2) inserted by s.13].

- The duties imposed by s.23ZA(2) are to be discharged in accordance with the *CA 1989 (Visits to Former Looked After Children in Detention (England) Regulations 2010* (SI 2797) made for the purposes of this section by the Secretary of State and are subject to any requirement imposed by or under an enactment applicable to the place in which the person to whom this section applies is accommodated (e.g. in custody or detained under the Mental Health Act) [s.23ZA(3)].

- The regulations (summarised below) make provision about the:
  - Frequency of visits
  - Circumstances in which a person to whom this section applies must be visited by a representative and
  - Functions of a representative [s.23ZA(4)].

- In choosing a representative, a local authority must satisfy itself that the person chosen has the necessary skills and experience to perform the functions of a representative [s.23ZA(5)].

Local Authority General Duties towards Looked After Children

Visits to Former Looked After Children in Detention (England) Regulations 2010

- The regulations apply to a child (A) who was looked after by a local authority but *ceases to be so as a result of being detained pursuant to a court order* in a young offender institution (YOI), secure training centre (STC) or a secure children's home [reg.3(1)].

    NB. These regulations do not apply to a 'relevant child' as per s.23A CA 1989, i.e. one who has already ceased to be looked after.

- The responsible local authority must ensure that their representative R visits A:

    - Within 10 days of A first being detained, in so far as is reasonably practicable and
    - Thereafter, whenever reasonably requested to do so by A, a member of staff of the institution where A is detained, any parent of or any other person with parental responsibility for A or the relevant youth offending (YOT) manager [reg.4(1)].

- The responsible local authority may arrange for R to make such additional visits to A having regard to any recommendations made by R in accordance with reg.6(1)(b) [reg.4(2)].

- On each visit R must speak to A in private unless A, being of sufficient age and understanding, refuses, R considers it inappropriate to do so having regard to A's age and understanding, or R is unable to do so [reg.5].

- R must provide a written report of each visit which must include:

    - R's assessment, having regard to A's wishes and feelings as to whether A's welfare is being adequately safeguarded and promoted whilst in detention
    - R's recommendations as to the timing and frequency of any further visits by R
    - Any other arrangements which R considers should be put in place with a view to promoting contact between A and her/his family or in order to safeguard and promote A's welfare

- R's assessment as to how A's welfare should be adequately safeguarded and promoted following release from detention, in particular, whether A will need to be provided with accommodation on release by the responsible authority or another local authority; whether any other services should be provided by the responsible local authority or another local authority in the exercise of its duties under the CA 1989 [reg.6(1)].

■ R's assessment must, unless it is not reasonably practicable to do or it is not consistent with A's welfare, take into account the views of:

- Any parent of or any other person with parental responsibility for A
- Appropriate members of staff of the institution in which A is detained [reg.6(2)].

■ The responsible local authority must give a copy of the report to:

- A, unless it would be inappropriate to do so
- Any parent or person with parental responsibility, unless to do so would not be in A's best interests
- The governor, director or registered manager of the institution where A is being detained
- The relevant YOT manager
- When different from the responsible local authority, the local authority in whose area A is detained
- Any other person whom the responsible authority considers should be given a copy of the report having regard to R's assessment [reg.6(3)].

■ When making arrangements in accordance with s.23ZA(2)(b) for appropriate advice, support and assistance to be available to A between R's visits, the responsible authority must ensure that:

- The arrangements are appropriate having regard to A's age and understanding, give due consideration to A's religious persuasion, racial origin, cultural and linguistic background and to any disability A may have
- C's wishes and feelings about the arrangements are ascertained and taken into consideration

- As far as is reasonably practicable, having regard to A's age and understanding, A knows how to seek appropriate advice, support and assistance from the authority [reg.7].

Child with a Disability: Additional Duties

- Work with children who have a disability should be based on the principles that:
  - They are children first and their disability is a secondary, albeit significant, issue
  - The aim should be to promote access to the same range of services for all.

- Local authorities:
  - Must, so far as is practical, when they provide accommodation for a disabled child, ensure that the accommodation is suitable for her/his needs [s.22C(8) CA 1989]
  - Must maintain, for forward planning purposes, a register of children who have a disability [Sch. 2 para.2 CA 1989]
  - May assess a child's needs for the purpose of the Children Act at the same time as any assessment under certain other Acts, e.g. Education Act 1996 [Sch.2 para. 3 CA 1989]
  - Must provide services for children who have a disability which are designed to minimise the effects of the disability and give them the opportunity to lead as normal lives as possible [Sch.2 para. 6 CA 1989].

- The rights of disabled children to consent to or refuse assessment/treatment or access their records is limited only by the general conditions about sufficient understanding which apply to other children.

CARE PLANNING, PLACEMENT & CASE REVIEW (ENGLAND) REGULATIONS 2010 (AS AMENDED)

Care Planning, Placement & Case Review (England) Regulations 2010 (as amended)

Interpretations & Application of CPP & CR (England) Regulations 2010 (as amended)

- For the purposes of these regulations, the following terms are to be interpreted as described here.
- 'Appropriate person' means:
  - P, if C is to live or lives with P
  - F, if C is to be placed or is placed with F
  - If C is to be placed, or is placed in a children's home, the person registered under Part 2 Care Standards Act 2000 as carrying on or managing the home
  - If C is placed or to be placed in accordance with other arrangements under s.22C(6)(d), the person who will be responsible for C at the accommodation on behalf of the responsible authority (if any).
- 'Area authority' means the local authority for the area in which C is placed or to be placed, if this is different from the responsible authority.
- 'C' means a child who is 'looked after' by the responsible authority.
- 'Care plan' means the plan for the future care of C prepared in accordance with regs.4–8 of these regulations.
- 'Case record' has the meaning given in reg.49 (see pp68-9).
- 'Connected person' means a relative (grandparent, brother, sister, uncle or aunt – of full or half blood, or by marriage/civil partnership or stepparent), friend or other person connected with C.
- 'Director of Children's Services' means the officer of the responsible authority appointed for purposes of s.18 Children Act 2004.
- 'F' means a person who is approved as a local authority foster parent and with whom it is proposed to place C, or as the case may be, C is placed.
- 'Health plan' means the arrangements made by the responsible authority to meet C's health care needs.

- 'Independent visitor' means the person appointed to be C's visitor under s.23ZB CA 1989 and reg.47.
- 'IRO' means the independent reviewing officer appointed for C's case under s.25A(1); the 'officer' means the director of children's services or other senior officer of the responsible authority nominated in writing by the director to act on behalf of her/him.
- 'P' means:
  - A person who is C's parent
  - A person who is not C's parent but who has gained parental responsibility for C or
  - If C is in the care of the responsible authority and there was a Residence Order/Child Arrangements Order determining with whom the child shall live in force for C immediately before the Care Order was made, a person in whose favour that order was made.

Long Term Foster Placement

- A 'long term foster placement' means an arrangement made by the responsible authority for C to be placed with F where:
  - C's plan for permanence is foster care
  - F has agreed to act as C's foster carer until C ceases to be looked after and
  - The responsible authority has confirmed the nature of the arrangement to F, P and C (any reference to the responsible authority placing C in such a placement includes, if C is already placed there, leaving her/him with F in a long term foster placement [reg.2(1) CPP&CR Regulations as amended by Care Planning and Fostering (Miscellaneous Amendments) (England) Regulations 2015].
- 'Pathway plan' has the meaning of s.23E CA 1989, i.e. a plan setting out for:
  - 'Eligible children', the advice, assistance and support which the local authority intends to provide while it is looking after the person and later (including when s/he may cease to be looked after) and

- 'Relevant children', the advice, assistance and support the local authority intends to provide under Part III CA 1989.
- 'Personal adviser' means the personal adviser arranged for C under para.19C Sch.2 CA 1989.
- 'Personal education plan' means the arrangements made by the responsible authority to meet C's educational and training needs.
- 'Placement' means the arrangements made by the responsible authority to provide for C's accommodation and maintenance by any of the means specified in s.22C CA 1989 or arrangements for C to live with a person with parental responsibility.
- 'Placement plan' – see reg.9(1) on page 29.
- 'Plan for permanence' has the meaning given in regulation 5(a) of the CPP&CR (England) Regulations 2010 as amended – see section below on Arrangements for Looking after a Child.
- 'R' means the representative of the responsible authority who visits C in accordance with arrangements made by it under s.23ZA CA 1989.
- The 'responsible authority' means the local authority that looks after C.
- 'Working day' means any day other than a Saturday or Sunday, Christmas Day or Good Friday or a bank holiday in England and Wales.

Note: that these regs do not apply to a child who has been placed for adoption [reg.3].

Arrangements for Looking After a Child

Care Planning [Reg.4 CPP&CR (England) Regulations 2010]

- If a child (C) is not in the care of the responsible authority and a care plan for her/him has not already been prepared, the responsible authority

Care Planning, Placement & Case Review (England) Regulations 2010 (as amended)

must assess C's needs for its services to achieve or maintain a reasonable standard of health or development, and prepare such a plan [reg.4(1)].

- *Except* in the case of a child to whom s.31A applies (i.e. one subject to Care Proceedings in which case the court will set the time within which the care plan must be prepared), the care plan must be prepared *before* C is first placed by the responsible authority or, if it is not practicable to do so, within 10 working days of the start of the first placement [reg.4(2)].

- When assessing C's needs under reg.4(1), the responsible authority must consider whether the placement provided for C meets the requirements of Part 3 of the 1989 Act, i.e. will enable the discharge of all the duties in Part 3 [reg.4(3)].

- Unless reg.4(5) applies, the care plan should so far as is reasonably practicable be agreed by the responsible authority with:

  - Any parent of C's and any person who is not C's parent but who has parental responsibility for her/him, or
  - If there is no such person, the person who was caring for C immediately before the responsible authority arranged a placement for C [reg.4(4)].

- If C is aged 16 or over and agrees to be provided with accommodation under s.20(1) CA 1989 as amended, the care plan should be agreed with C by the responsible authority [reg.4(5)].

Preparation & Content of Care Plan [Regs.5 & 6 CPP&CR (England) Regulations 2010]

- The care plan must include a record of the following:

  - Long term plan for C's upbringing ('the plan for permanence')
  - Arrangements made by the responsible authority to meet C's needs in relation to health (inc. information set out in para.1 Sch.1 of these regulations (the 'health plan', see below) education and training, inc. information in para.2 of Sch.1 (the 'personal education plan', see below); emotional and behavioural development, identity, with particular regard to C's religious persuasion, racial origin and cultural and linguistic background, family and social relationships and in

particular the information set out in para.3 of Sch.1 (see below); social presentation, and self-care skills
- Except in a case when C is in the care of the responsible authority but is not provided with accommodation by it by any of the means referred to in s.22C, the placement plan
- Name of the independent reviewing officer (IRO)
- Details of the wishes and feelings of the persons listed in s.22(4) about the 'arrangements' referred to above, the placement plan that have been ascertained and considered in accordance with s.22(4) and (5) and the wishes and feelings of those persons in relation to any change, or proposed change, to the care plan [reg.5].
- The fact that C is a victim of trafficking or an UASC (inserted by reg.3 of the Care Planning and Care Leavers (Amendment) Regulations 2014).

■ The responsible authority must keep C's care plan under review in accordance with Part 6 of these regulations (Case Reviews) and, if it is of the opinion some change is required, it must revise the plan or make a new plan accordingly [reg.6(1)].

■ Unless otherwise allowed by these regulations, the responsible authority must not make any significant change to the care plan unless the proposed change has first been considered at a review of C's case [reg.6(2)].

■ The responsible authority must give a copy of the care plan to:
- C, unless it would not be appropriate to do so having regard to her/his age and understanding
- P
- The IRO
- If C is to be placed, or is placed with F, the fostering service provider that approved F in accordance with the fostering regulations
- If C is to be placed, or is placed in a children's home, to the person registered under Part 2 Care Standards Act in respect of that home
- If C is to be placed, or is placed, in accordance with other arrangements under s.22C(6)(d), to the person who will be responsible for C at the accommodation [reg.6(3)].

Care Planning, Placement & Case Review (England) Regulations 2010 (as amended)

- The responsible authority may decide not to give a copy of the care plan, or a full copy of the care plan to P if to do so would put C at risk of significant harm [reg.6(4)].

Information to be included in the Health Plan [Sch.1 para.1 in Support of Reg.5 CPP&CR (England) Regulations 2010]

- C's state of health including physical, emotional and mental health [Sch.1 para.1(1)].
- C's health history including, as far as practicable, C's family's health history [Sch.1 para.1(2)].
- The effect of C's health and health history on C's development [Sch.1 para.1(3)].
- Existing arrangements for C's medical and dental care, appropriate to C's needs, including:
  - Routine checks of C's general state of health, including dental health
  - Treatment and monitoring for identified health (including physical, emotional and mental health) or dental care needs
  - Preventive measures such as vaccination and immunisation
  - Screening for defects of vision or hearing; and
  - Advice and guidance on promoting health and effective personal care [Sch.1 para.1(4)].
- Any planned changes to the arrangements [Sch.1 para.1(5)].
- The role of the appropriate person, and of any other person who cares for C, in promoting C's health [Sch.1.para.1(6)].

Information to be included in the Personal Education Plan [Sch.1 para.2 in support of Reg.5 CPP&CR (England) Regulations 2010]

- C's educational and training history including information about educational institutions attended and C's attendance and conduct record; academic and other achievements; and C's special educational needs, if any [Sch.1 para.2(1)].

- Existing arrangements for C's education and training including details of any special educational provision and any other provision made to meet C's particular educational or training needs and to promote C's educational achievement [Sch.1 para.2(2)] including the name and contact details of the person responsible for discharging the LA's duty to promote educational achievement of LAC (inserted by reg.7 of 2013 Amends).

- Any planned change to existing arrangements for C's education or training and if any changes are necessary, provision made to minimise disruption to that education or training achievement [Sch.1 para.2(3)].

- C's leisure interests [Sch.1 para.2 (4)].

- The role of the appropriate person and of any other person who cares for C in promoting C's educational achievements and leisure interests [Sch.1 para.2 (5)].

    NB. s.99 CAF 2014 introduces an obligation for each local authority to appoint at least one officer from its own or another English local authority to ensure promotion of the educational achievement of its looked after children.

Family & Social Relationships [Sch.1 para.3 in Support of Reg.5 CPP&CR (England) Regulations 2010] & Statutory Guidance: Volume 2 revised para. 2.44

- If C has a sibling for whom the responsible authority or another authority is providing accommodation and the children have not been placed together the arrangements made to promote contact between them, so far as is consistent with C's welfare [Sch.1 para.3(1)].

- If C is looked after by, but is not in the care of, the responsible authority details of any order relating to C made under s.8 CA 1989 [Sch.1 para.3(2)].

- If C is a child in the care of the responsible authority, details of any order relating to C made under s.34 (parental contact etc with children in care) [Sch.1 para.3(3)].

- Any other arrangements made to promote and maintain contact in accordance with para.15 of Sch.2 so far as is reasonably practicable and consistent with C's welfare between C and any parent of her/him; any person who is not a parent but has parental responsibility for C and any other connected persons [Sch.1 para.3(4)].
- If s.23ZB(1) (appointment of independent visitor) applies, the arrangements made to appoint an independent visitor for C, or if s.23ZB(6) applies (appointment of independent visitor not made when child objects) that fact [Sch.1. para.3(5)].

Health Care [Reg.7 CPP&CR (England) Regulations 2010]

- Before C is first placed by it, or if that is not reasonably practicable before the first review of C's case, the responsible authority must make arrangements for a registered medical practitioner to:
  - Carry out an assessment of C's state of health
  - Provide a written report of the assessment, addressing the matters specified in para.1 of Sch.1 to these regulations (i.e. the health plan, see above) as soon as reasonably practicable [reg.7(1)].
- Reg.7(1) does not apply if in the three months immediately preceding placement, an assessment of C's state of health has been carried out and the responsible authority has obtained a written report that meets the requirements of that paragraph [reg.7(2)].
- The responsible authority must make arrangements for a registered medical practitioner or a registered nurse or registered midwife acting under the supervision of a registered medical practitioner, to review C's state of health and provide a written report of each review, addressing the matters specified in the 'health plan' at least every:
  - six months before C's fifth birthday, and
  - 12 months after C's fifth birthday [reg.7(3)].
- Reg.7(1) and (3) do not apply if C refuses consent to the assessment, being of sufficient understanding to do so [reg.7(4)].

Care Planning, Placement & Case Review (England) Regulations 2010 (as amended)

- The responsible authority must take all reasonable steps to ensure that C is provided with appropriate health care services, in accordance with the health plan, including:
  - Medical and dental care and treatment, and
  - Advice and guidance on health, personal care and health promotion issues [reg.7(5)].

Contact with a Child in Care [Reg.8 CPP&CR (England) Regulations 2010] & Statutory Guidance: Volume 2 para.2.95

- When considering whether contact between C and any person mentioned in paras. (a)–(d) of s.34(1) CA 1989 is consistent with C's welfare, the responsible authority must have regard to C's care plan [reg.82A].

- Reg.8 applies if C is in the care of the responsible authority and the responsible authority has decided under s.34(6) CA 1989 (refusal of contact as a matter of urgency) to refuse to allow contact that would otherwise be required by virtue of s.34(1) or an order under s.34 (parental contact etc with a child in care) [reg.8(1)].

- The responsible authority must immediately send written notification to the following persons of the information specified in reg.8(3) below:
  - C, unless it would not be appropriate to do so having regard to C's age and understanding
  - P
  - If, immediately before the Care Order was made a person had care of C by virtue of an order made in exercise of the High Court's inherent jurisdiction with respect to children, that person
  - Any other person whose wishes and feelings the responsible authority consider to be relevant, and
  - The IRO [reg.8(2)].

- The information specified in reg.8(2) above is:
  - The responsible authority's decision
  - Date of the decision
  - Reasons for the decision
  - Duration of the decision (if applicable), and

Care Planning, Placement & Case Review (England) Regulations 2010 (as amended)

- Remedies available in case of dissatisfaction [reg.8(3)].

■ The responsible authority may depart from the terms of any order made under s.34 CA 1989 by agreement with the person in relation to whom the order is made, provided that:

  - C, being of sufficient understanding, also agrees, and
  - Written notification of the specified information is sent within five working days to the persons specified in reg.8(2) [reg.8(4)].

■ If the responsible authority has decided to vary or suspend any arrangement made (otherwise than under an order under s.34) with a view to affording any person contact with C, it must immediately give written notification containing the specified information to the persons listed in reg.8(2) [reg.8(5)].

■ The responsible authority must record any decision made under this regulation in C's care plan [reg.8(6)].

Placements: General Provisions

Placement Plan [Reg.9 CPP&CR Regulations 2010]

■ Subject to reg.9(2) or now redundant transitional provision (4), before making arrangements in accordance with s.22C CA 1989 for C's accommodation the responsible authority must:

  - Prepare a plan for the placement ('the placement plan') that sets out how the placement will contribute to meeting C's needs, and
  - Includes all the matters specified in Sch.2 (reproduced below) as are applicable, having regard to the nature of the placement and
  - Ensure that C's wishes and feelings have been ascertained and given due consideration and that the IRO has been informed [reg.9(1)].

■ If it is not reasonably practicable to make the placement plan before making the placement, it must be made within five working days thereafter [reg.9(2)].

Care Planning, Placement & Case Review (England) Regulations 2010 (as amended)

- The placement plan must be agreed with, and signed by, the appropriate person [reg.9(3)].

Particulars that must be included in C's Placement Plan [Sch.2 in Support of Reg.9 CPP&CR (England) Regulations 2010] as amended by the Fostering Services (England) Regulations 2011 & Care Planning Placement and Case Review and Fostering Services (Miscellaneous Amendments) Regulations 2013 and the Care Planning and Fostering (Miscellaneous Amendments) (England) Regulations 2015

- How on a day to day basis C will be cared for and her/his welfare safeguarded and promoted by the appropriate person [Sch.2 para.1(1)].

- Any arrangements made for contact between C and any parent of C's and any person who is not C's parent but who has parental responsibility for C, and between C and other connected persons inc. if appropriate, the reasons why contact with any such person would not be reasonably practicable or would not be consistent with C's welfare; if C is not in the care of the responsible authority, details of any order made under s.8; if C is in the care of the responsible authority, details of any order relating to C made under s.34 (parental contact etc with children in care); the arrangements for notifying any changes in contact arrangements [Sch.2 para.1(2)].

- The arrangements made for C's health (including physical, emotional and mental health) and dental care and for her/his education and training [Sch.2 para (3);(4) CPP&CR Regulations 2010 as amended], and if C is placed in a long term foster placement, that fact [Sch.2 para.3(1)(1ZA) introduced by reg.9 Care Planning and Fostering (Miscellaneous Amendments) (England) Regulations 2015].

- The respective responsibilities of the responsible authority, C's parents and any person who is not C's parent but who has parental responsibility for her/him [Sch.2 para.3(4) as substituted].

- Any delegation of authority to make decisions about C's care and upbringing by the persons mentioned above (as appropriate) to the responsible authority, F and, if C is placed in a children's home, the appropriate person, in relation to the following matters and identifying any matters about which they consider that C may make a decision:

- Medical and dental treatment
- Education
- Leisure and home life
- Faith and religious observance
- Use of social media
- Any other matters they consider appropriate [reg.(4A);(B)].

■ The arrangements made for R to visit C in accordance with Part 5 (visits by the responsible authority's representative etc), the frequency of visits and the arrangements made for advice, support and assistance to be available to C between visits in accordance with reg.31 (advice, support and assistance for the child) [Sch.2 para.1(5)].

■ If an independent visitor is appointed, the arrangements made for them to visit C [Sch.2 para.1(6)].

■ The circumstances in which the placement may be terminated and C removed from the appropriate person's care in accordance with reg.14 [Sch.2 para.1(7)].

■ The name and contact details of:

- The IRO
- C's independent visitor (if one is appointed)
- R and
- If C is an 'eligible child', the personal adviser appointed for C [Sch.2 para.1(8)].

■ Additional information to be included if C is placed under 'placement with parents etc':

- Details of support and services to be provided to P during the placement [Sch.2 para. 2(1)].
- The obligation on P to notify the responsible authority of any relevant change in circumstances, including any intention to change address, any changes in the household in which C lives, and of any serious incident involving C

- The obligation on P to ensure that any information relating to C or C's family or any other person given in confidence to P in connection with the placement is kept confidential and that such information is not disclosed to any person without the consent of the responsible authority [Sch.2 para.2(3)].
- The circumstances in which it is necessary to obtain in advance the approval of the responsible authority for C to live in a household other than P's household [Sch. 2 para.2(4)].
- The arrangements for requesting a change to the agreement [Sch.2 para.2(5)].
- The circumstances in which the placement will be terminated in accordance with reg.19(c)(ii) (child placed with parents etc before assessment completed) [Sch.2 para.2(6)].

■ Additional information to be included if C is placed with F, in a children's home or in other arrangements:

- The type of accommodation to be provided, its address and, when C is placed in other arrangements under s.22C(6)(d), the name of the person who will be responsible for C at that accommodation on behalf of the responsible authority (if any) [Sch.2 para.3(1)].
- Where the responsible authority has, or is notified of child protection concerns relating to C, or C has gone missing from placement or from any previous placement, the day to day arrangements put in place by the appropriate person to keep her/him safe [Sch.2 para.3(1A) as inserted by Children's Homes and Looked After Children (Miscellaneous Amendments) (England) Regulations 2013.
- C's personal history, religious persuasion, cultural and linguistic background, and racial origin [Sch.2 para.3(2)].
- If C is looked after but is not in the care of the responsible authority – the respective responsibilities of the responsible authority and C's parents or any person who is not C's parent but who has parental responsibility for C; any delegation of responsibility to the responsible authority for C's day to day care there has been by C's parents or any person who is not C's parent but has parental responsibility for C; the expected duration of the arrangements and the steps which should be taken to bring the arrangements to an end, inc. arrangements for C to

return to live with C's parents or any person who is not C's parent but who has parental responsibility for C; and if C is aged 16 or over and agrees to being provided with accommodation under s.20, that fact [Sch.2 para.3(3)].
- The circumstances in which it is necessary to obtain in advance, the responsible authority's approval for C to take part in school trips or to stay away from the placement [Sch.2 para.3(4)].
- The responsible authority's arrangements for the financial support of C during the placement [Sch.2 para.3(5)].
- If C is placed with F, the obligation on F to comply with the terms of the foster care agreement made under reg.27(5)(b) of the Fostering Services Regulations [Sch.2 para.3(6)].

Foster Carer's Delegated Authority [Volume 2 Statutory Guidance: paras. 3.192-3.223 and Volume 4 Statutory Guidance: revised paras. 3.9-3.24]

- Volumes 2 and 4 confirm that, except when there are identified factors which dictate to the contrary, carers should be given delegated authority to make day to day decisions about health, education, leisure, etc.

- Each local authority should have a published policy setting out its approach to delegation.

- In making decisions about whether or not to permit a looked after child to stay overnight with a friend or to have a holiday with their friends or with relatives of their foster carers, or to go on a school trip, foster carers and responsible authorities should consider the following factors:

  - Whether there are any relevant restrictions contained for exceptional reasons in the child's care plan, including the placement plan
  - Whether there are any court orders which restrict the child from making a particular overnight stay, visit or holiday
  - Whether there are any factors in the child's past experiences or behaviour which would preclude the overnight stay, visit or holiday
  - Whether there are any grounds for concern that the child may be at significant risk in the household concerned or from the activities proposed

- The age and level of understanding of the child concerned
- What is known about the reasons for the overnight stay, visit or holiday
- The length of the stay.

■ If in doubt about the appropriate decision or if there is reason to consider that a child may be at specific risk in staying in a particular household, the foster carers should consult the responsible authority for advice. The child and her/his carers should always be told of the criteria that will be used to make decisions about overnight stays, visits and holidays.

■ Foster carers should always have contact details for the household in which the child will be staying. They should also make contact with the household beforehand, as would any good parent, to assist in assessing the request and to confirm arrangements and to ensure that the household where the child will be staying have, in turn, the contact details of the foster carer/s.

■ There is *no* statutory duty for Disclosure and Barring Service (DBS) disclosures to be sought in relation to adults in a private household where a child may stay overnight or visit, or who the child may accompany on a holiday or on a school trip. DBS checks should not normally be sought as a pre-condition.

■ There is no requirement that where a looked after child visits or spends a holiday with their foster carer's friends or relative that the individual must be approved as a local authority foster carer, as the child will remain formally placed with their usual foster carers.

NB. The Fostering Network has a useful 'tool' at https://www.fostering. net/sites/www.fostering.net/files/public/resources/good-practice- guidance/delegated-authority-decision-support-tool.pdf.

Avoidance of Disruption in Education [Reg.10 CPP&CR (England) Regulations 2010]

■ Subject to reg.10(2) and (3), if C is a registered pupil at a school in the 4th key stage, a decision to make any change to her/his placement that would have the effect of disrupting the arrangements made for C's

Care Planning, Placement & Case Review (England) Regulations 2010 (as amended)

education must not be put into effect until it has been approved by a 'nominated officer' [reg.10(1)].

- Before approving a decision under reg.10(1), the nominated officer must first be satisfied that:
  - C's wishes and feelings have been ascertained, and given due consideration to
  - The educational provision made for C at the placement will promote her/his educational achievement and is consistent with C's personal education plan
  - The designated teacher at the school had been consulted and
  - The IRO had been consulted [reg.10(2)].

  NB. The 'designated teacher' for a maintained school is the member of staff designated by the governing body in accordance with s.20(1) CYPA 2008. Academies, City Technology Colleges and City Colleges for the Technology of the Arts are required by their funding arrangements to have a designated teacher. The Designated Teacher (Looked After Pupils etc) (England) Regulations 2009 SI 2009/1538 prescribe the qualifications and experience of the designated teacher.

- Reg.10(1) does not apply in any case when the responsible authority terminates C's placement in accordance with reg.14(3) (termination of placements) or it is necessary for any other reason to change C's placement and in such a case the responsible authority must make appropriate arrangements to promote C's educational achievement as soon as reasonably practicable [reg.10(3)].

- In any case not falling within reg.10(1), but where the responsible authority proposes making any change to C's placement that would have the effect of disrupting the arrangements made for C's education or training, the responsible authority must ensure that other arrangements are made for C's education or training that meets C's needs and are consistent with C's personal education plan [reg.10(4)].

NB. In this regulation '4th key stage' means a pupil in the 4th stage for purposes of Part 6 or 7 of the Education Act 2002; 'registered pupil' has the meaning given in s.20(7) Children and Young Persons Act 2008 and 'school' has the meaning given in s.4 Education Act 1996 (i.e. an educational institution outside further and higher education sectors for providing primary and/or secondary education).

Placements out of Area [Regs.11–12 CPP&CR (England) Regulations 2010]

- Subject to regs.11(2)–(4) CPP&CR Regulations 2010, a decision to place C outside the area of the responsible authority (including a placement outside England):
  - Must not be put into effect until it has been approved by a nominated officer or
  - In the case of a proposed placement which is also 'at a distance', must not be put into effect until it has been approved by the director of children's services (DCS) [reg.11(1) as substituted by reg.18 Children's Homes and Looked After Children (Miscellaneous Amendments) (England) Regulations 2013].

- Before approving such a decision the nominated officer, or as the case may be, DCS must be satisfied that:
  - The placement is the most appropriate one available for C and consistent with her/his care plan
  - C's relatives have been consulted where appropriate
  - The IRO has been consulted [reg.11(2)].

- In the case of a decision being made by a nominated officer, the area authority must be notified and in the case of a decision requiring a DCS the area authority must be consulted and have been provided with a copy of C's care plan [reg.11(2)(d)(ii)].

- Reg.11(1) and (2) do *not* apply to a decision to place C outside the area of the responsible authority:
  - With F who is a 'connected person'
  - With F who is approved as a local authority foster parent by the responsible authority [reg.11(4)].

Care Planning, Placement & Case Review (England) Regulations 2010 (as amended)

- Reg.12 applies if C is in the care of the responsible authority, and the responsible authority makes arrangements to place her/him outside England and Wales in accordance with the provisions of para.19 of Sch.2 (placement of a child in care outside England and Wales) [reg.12(1)].

- The responsible authority must take steps to ensure that, so far as is reasonably practicable, requirements corresponding with the requirements which would have applied under these Regulations had C been placed in England, are complied with [reg.12(2)].

- The responsible authority must include in the care plan details of the arrangements made to supervise C's placement [reg.12(3)].

Notifications of Placements [Reg.13 CPP&CR (England) Regulations 2010]

- Subject to reg.13(3), the responsible authority must give written notice to the persons listed in reg.13(2) below of the arrangements for C's placement *before* the placement is made or, if immediate placement is necessary, within five working days after the placement is made, unless it is not reasonably practicable to do so [reg.13(1)].

- The persons referred to in reg.13(1) are:
  - C, unless it would not be appropriate to do so having regard to C's age and understanding
  - Any parent of C's and any person who is not C's parent but who has parental responsibility for C (or, if C is in the care of the responsible authority and there was a Residence/Child Arrangements Order in force on C immediately before the Care Order was made, a person in whose favour that Order was made)
  - If C is in the care of the responsible authority, any person who is allowed contact with C under s.34(1) CA 1989 and any person who has contact with C by virtue of an order under s.34 of that Act (contact with a child in care by parents etc)
  - If C is looked after, but is *not* in the care of the responsible authority, any person who has contact with C pursuant to an order made under s.8

Care Planning, Placement & Case Review (England) Regulations 2010 (as amended)

- Any person who was caring for C immediately before the arrangements were made
- The Clinical Commissioning Group (or in the case of a child living or to be placed in Wales, the local Health Board) for the area in which C is living and, if different, for the area in which C is to be placed
- C's registered medical practitioner and, when applicable, the registered medical practitioner with whom C is to be registered during the placement
- Any educational institution attended by, or person providing education or training for, C, and
- The IRO [reg.13(2)].

■ The responsible authority may decide not to give notice to any or all of the persons listed in bullets 2–5 above if to do so would place C at risk of significant harm [reg.13(3)].

■ In the case of a placement outside the area of a responsible authority (including a placement outside England):

- The responsible authority must give written notification to the area authority of the arrangements for C's placement before the placement is made, or if it is made in an emergency, within five working days of the start of the placement unless not reasonably practical to do so, and
- The notification must include details of the responsible authority's assessment of C's needs and the reasons why the placement is the most suitable for responding to them, and a copy of her/his care plan (unless this has already been provided to the area by virtue of reg.11(2)(d)(ii) [reg.13(4) introduced by reg.19 Children's Homes and Looked After Children (Miscellaneous Amendments) (England) Regulations 2013].

Termination of Placement by the Responsible Authority [Reg.14 CPP&CR (England) Regulations 2010]

■ Subject to regs.14(3) and 14(5) the responsible authority may *only* terminate C's placement following a review of C's case in accordance with Part 6 of these regulations [reg.14(1)].

Care Planning, Placement & Case Review (England) Regulations 2010 (as amended)

- Subject to reg.14(3), before terminating C's placement, the responsible authority must:
  - Make other arrangements for C's accommodation, in accordance with s.22C
  - Inform the IRO
  - So far as is reasonably practicable, give written notice of its intention to terminate it to all the persons to whom notice of the placement was given under reg.13; the person who is providing the placement; if C is placed in the area of another local authority, the area authority [reg.14(2)].

- If there is an immediate risk of significant harm to C or to protect others from serious injury, the responsible authority must terminate C's placement and in those circumstances:
  - Reg.14(1) does not apply
  - The responsible authority must make other arrangements for C's accommodation, in accordance with s.22C and inform the IRO as soon as reasonably practicable [reg.14(3)].

- If it is not reasonably practicable to notify any person in accordance with reg.14(2), then the responsible authority must give written notice to that person within 10 working days of the placement's termination [reg.14(4)].

- Regulation 14 does *not* apply if C's placement is terminated under reg.19(c) (removal of child placed with a parent), reg.23(2) (removal of child from an 'emergency placement' with a foster carer outside the terms of approval) or reg.25(6) (removal from a friend/relative who has temporary approval) nor if s.22D (review of child's case before making alternative arrangements for accommodation) applies [reg.14(5)].

Provision for Different Types of Placement: Placement of a Child in Care with Parents etc

Application [Reg.15 CPP&CR (England) Regulations 2010]

- Regs.15–21 apply if C is in the care of the responsible authority and it, acting in accordance with s.22C(2), proposes to place C with P [reg.15].

  NB. Nothing in regs.15–21 requires the responsible authority to remove C from P's care if C is living with P before a placement decision is made about her/him [reg.15(2)].

Effect of Contact Order [Reg.16 CPP&CR (England) Regulations 2010]

- The responsible authority must not place C with P if to do so would be incompatible with any order made by the court under s.34 CA 1989 (parental contact with children in care etc) [reg.16].

Assessment of P's Suitability to Care for a Child [Reg.17 CPP&CR (England) Regulations 2010]

- Before deciding to place C with P, the responsible authority must:
  - Assess the suitability of P to care for C inc. the suitability of the proposed accommodation and all other persons aged 18 and over who are members of the household
  - Take into account all the matters set out in Sch.3 (reproduced below) in making its assessment
  - Consider whether, in all the circumstances and taking into account the services to be provided by the responsible authority, the placement will safeguard and promote C's welfare and meet C's needs set out in the care plan and
  - Review C's case in accordance with Part 6 [reg.17].

Care Planning, Placement & Case Review (England) Regulations 2010 (as amended)

Matters to be taken into Account when Assessing Suitability of P to Care for C [Sch.3 CPP&CR (England) Regulations 2010]

- P's capacity to care for children and in particular in relation to C to:
  - Provide for C's physical needs and appropriate medical and dental care
  - Protect C adequately from harm or danger, and from any person who presents a risk of harm to C
  - Ensure that the home environment is safe for C
  - Ensure that C's emotional needs are met and C is provided with a positive sense of self, including any particular needs arising from C's religious persuasion, racial origin and cultural and linguistic background, and any disability C may have
  - Promote C's learning and intellectual development through encouragement, cognitive stimulation and the promotion of educational success and social opportunities
  - Enable C to regulate C's emotions and behaviour, including by modelling appropriate behaviour and interactions with others; and
  - Provide a stable family environment to enable C to develop and maintain secure attachments to P and other persons who care for C.

- P's state of health, including P's physical and mental and emotional health and medical history including any current or past issues of domestic violence, substance misuse and mental health problems.

- P's family relationships and composition of P's household, including particulars of:
  - Identity of all other members of the household, including their age and the nature of their relationship with P and with each other, including any sexual relationship
  - Any relationship with any person who is a parent of C
  - Other adults not being members of the household who are likely to have regular contact with C, and
  - Any current or previous domestic violence between members of the household, including P.

- P's family history, including particulars of:

- P's childhood and upbringing including the strengths and difficulties of P's parents or other persons who cared for P
  - P's relationships with P's parents and siblings, and their relationships with each other
  - P's educational achievement and of any specific learning difficulty or disability, and
  - Chronology of significant life events, and
  - Particulars of other relatives and their relationships with C and P.

- Particulars of any criminal offences of which P has been convicted or in respect of which P has been cautioned.

- P's past and present employment and other sources of income.

- The nature of the neighbourhood in which P's home is situated and resources available in the community to support C and P [Sch.3 para.1].

- In respect of members of the household aged 18 and over, so far as is practicable, all the particulars specified above should be taken into account *except* those relating to P's family history, her/his past and present employment and the nature of the neighbourhood in which P's home is situated [Sch.3 para.2].

Decision to Place a Child with Parent (P) etc [Reg.18 CPP&CR (England) Regulations 2010]

- The decision to place C with P must not be put into effect until it has been approved by a nominated officer and the responsible authority has prepared a placement plan for C [reg.18(1)].

- Before approving a decision under reg.18(1), the nominated officer must be satisfied that:
  - C's wishes and feelings have been ascertained and given due consideration
  - The requirements of reg.17 have been complied with
  - The placement will safeguard and promote C's welfare
  - The IRO has been consulted [reg.18(2)].

Care Planning, Placement & Case Review (England) Regulations 2010 (as amended)

Circumstances in which a Child May be Placed with a Parent etc (P) Before Assessment Completed [Reg.19 CPP&CR (England) Regulations 2010]

- If the nominated officer considers it to be necessary and consistent with C's welfare, the responsible authority may place C with P before its assessment under reg.17 ('the assessment') is completed, provided that it:

  - Arranges for P to be interviewed in order to obtain as much of the information specified in Sch.3 (see above) about P and the other persons living in P's household who are aged over 18 years as can be readily ascertained at that interview
  - Ensures that the assessment and review of C's case are completed in accordance with reg.17 within 10 working days of C being placed with P and
  - Ensures that a decision in accordance with reg.18 is made and approved within 10 working days after the assessment is completed and if the decision is to confirm the placement, review the placement plan and, if appropriate, amend it; and if the placement is not so confirmed, terminate it [reg.19].

Support for Parents etc [Reg.20 CPP&CR (England) Regulations 2010]

- If C is placed or to be placed with P, the responsible authority must provide such services and support to P as appear to it to be necessary so as to safeguard and promote C's welfare and must record details of such services and support in C's care plan [reg.20].

Provision for Different Types of Placement: Placement with Local Authority Foster Parents

Interpretation [Reg.21 CPP&CR (England) Regulations 2010]

- For the purposes of regs.21–26, 'registered person' is as defined in s.2(1) Fostering Services (England) Regulations 2011.

- If C is placed jointly with two persons, each of whom is approved as a local authority foster parent, any reference in these regulations to a local authority foster parent is to be interpreted as referring equally to both such persons and any requirement to be satisfied by or relating to a particular local authority foster parent must be satisfied by, or treated as relating to, both such persons [reg.21(2)].

Conditions to be Complied with Before Placing a Child with a Local Authority Foster Parent [Reg.22 CPP&CR (England) Regulations 2010]

- Reg.22 applies when the responsible authority proposes to place C with F [reg.22(1)].

- The responsible authority may only place C with F if:
  - F is approved by the responsible authority, or provided that the conditions specified in reg.22(3) are also satisfied, another fostering service provider
  - The terms of F's approval are consistent with the proposed placement, and
  - F has entered into a foster care agreement either with the responsible authority or with another fostering service provider in accordance with reg.27(5)(b) of the Fostering Services Regulations [reg.22(2)].

- The conditions referred to above are that:
  - The fostering service provider by whom F is approved consents to the placement

Care Planning, Placement & Case Review (England) Regulations 2010 (as amended)

- Any other local authority which currently has a child placed with F consents to the placement [reg.22(3)].

Conditions to be Complied with Before Placing C in a Long Term Placement [Reg.22B introduced by reg.4 Care Planning and Fostering (Miscellaneous Amendments) (England) Regulations 2015]

- If the responsible authority proposes to place C with F in a 'long term foster placement', it may do so only if:

  - The responsible authority has prepared a placement plan for C
  - The requirements of reg.9(1)(b)(i) (the placement plan – see above) have been complied with
  - The placement will safeguard and promote C's welfare
  - The IRO has been consulted
  - C's relatives have been consulted, where appropriate, and
  - F intends to act as C's foster carer until C ceases to be looked after

- The required frequency of visiting by the responsible authority representative (R) differs for long term foster placements – see below.

Emergency Placement with a Local Authority Foster Parent [Reg.23 CPP&CR (England) Regulations 2010]

- If it is necessary to place C in an emergency, the responsible authority may place C with any local authority foster parent who has been approved in accordance with the Fostering Services Regulations, even if the terms of that person's approval are not consistent with the placement, provided that the placement is for no longer than six working days [reg.23(1)].

- When the period of six working days referred to above has expired, the responsible authority must terminate the placement unless the terms of that person's approval have been amended to be consistent with the placement [reg.23(2)].

Temporary Approval of a Relative, Friend or Other Person Connected with C [Reg.24 CPP&CR (England) Regulations 2010]

■ If the responsible authority is satisfied that the most appropriate placement for C is with a connected person, even though s/he is not approved as a local authority foster carer, and that it is necessary for C to be placed there before that person's suitability to be a local authority foster carer has been assessed in accordance with the Fostering Services Regulations, it may approve that person as a local authority foster parent for a temporary period not exceeding 16 weeks ('temporary approval') *provided* that it first:

- Assesses the suitability of the connected person to care for C, including the suitability of the proposed accommodation, and all other persons aged 18 and over who are members of the household in which it is proposed that C will live
- When making its assessment, takes into account the matters set out in Sch.4 of these regulations reproduced below (assessment of suitability of a connected person to care for C),
- Consider whether, in all the circumstances and taking into account the services to be provided by the responsible authority, the proposed arrangements will safeguard and promote C's welfare and meet C's needs identified in the care plan, and
- Make immediate arrangements for the connected person's suitability to be a local authority foster parent to be assessed in accordance with the Fostering Services Regulations ('the full approval process') before the period of temporary approval expires [reg.24(1);(2)].

NB. In reg.24, 'connected person' means a relative, friend or other person connected with C [reg.24(3)]. There is no requirement for a DBS check to be completed prior to a reg.24 placement with a connected person.

Matters to be taken into Account when Assessing Suitability of a Connected Person to Care for C [Sch.4 CPP&CR (England) Regulations 2010 in support of reg.24]

■ In respect of the connected person:

- The nature and quality of any existing relationship with C.

- Their capacity to care for children and in particular in relation to C:
  - Provide for C's physical needs and appropriate medical and dental care
  - Protect C adequately from harm or danger, including from any person who presents a risk of harm to C
  - Ensure that the accommodation and home environment is suitable with regard to the age and developmental stage of C
  - Promote the learning and development of C
  - Provide a stable family environment which will promote secure attachments for C, including the promotion of positive contact with P and other connected persons unless to do so is not consistent with the duty to safeguard and promote C's welfare.

- Their state of health, including physical, emotional and mental health and medical history including any current or past issues of domestic violence, substance misuse or mental health problems.

- Their family relationships and composition of her/his household, including particulars of:
  - Identity of all other members of the household inc. their age and nature of their relationship with the connected person and each other, inc. any sexual relationship
  - Any relationship between C and other members of the household
  - Other adults not being members of the household who are likely to have regular contact with C and
  - Any current or previous domestic violence between members of the household inc. the connected person.

- Their family history inc:
  - Particulars of their childhood and upbringing including strengths and difficulties of their parents or other persons who care for them
  - Their relationships with their parents and siblings and relationships with each other
  - Their educational achievement and any specific learning difficulty or disability
  - A chronology of life events

- Particulars of other relatives and their relationship with C and the connected person.
- Particulars of any criminal offences of which they have been convicted or in respect of which cautioned.
- Past and present employment and other sources of income.
- The nature of the community in which their home is situated and resources available in the community to support C and the connected person.

Expiry of Temporary Approval [Reg.25 CPP&CR (England) Regulations 2010]

- Subject to reg.25(4), the responsible authority *may* extend the period of temporary approval of a connected person if either:
  - It is likely to expire before the full approval process is completed, or
  - The connected person, having undergone the full approval process, is *not* approved and seeks a review of the decision in accordance with regulations made under para.12F(1)(b) of Sch.2 CA 1989 [reg.25(1)] (application to the IRM).
- In a case when the temporary approval is likely to expire before the full approval process is completed, the responsible authority *may* extend the period of temporary approval once for a further period of up to eight weeks [reg.25(2)].
- In a case when a person is not approved and is seeking a review of that decision, the responsible authority may extend the period of temporary approval until the outcome of the review is known [reg.25(3)].
- In either case, before deciding whether to extend the temporary approval the responsible authority must first:
  - Consider whether placement with the connected person is still the most appropriate placement available
  - Seek the views of the fostering panel established by the fostering service provider in accordance with the Fostering Services Regulations, and

Care Planning, Placement & Case Review (England) Regulations 2010 (as amended)

- Inform the IRO [reg.25(4)].

■ A decision to extend temporary approval must be made by a nominated officer [reg.25(5)].

■ If the period of temporary approval and of any extension to that period expires and the connected person has not been approved as a local authority foster parent in accordance with the Fostering Services Regulations, the responsible authority must terminate the placement after first making other arrangements for C's accommodation [reg.25(6)].

Temporary Approval of Prospective Adopter as Foster Parent [Reg.25A CPP&CR (England) Regulations 2010] inserted by reg.3 Care Planning, Placement and Case Review and Fostering Services (Miscellaneous Amendments) Regulations 2013]

■ When the responsible authority is satisfied that the most appropriate placement for C is with a person who is not approved as a local authority foster parent but is an approved prospective adopter and it is in C's best interests to be placed with that person, it may approve her/him in relation to C for a 'temporary approval period', provided that it first:

- Assesses the suitability of that person to care for C as a foster parent
- Considers whether in all the circumstances and taking into account the services to be provided by the responsible authority, the proposed arrangements will safeguard and promote C's welfare and meet her/his needs as set out in the care plan.

■ The temporary approval period expires:

- On C's placement with the approved prospective adopter being terminated by the responsible authority
- On the approved prospective adopter's approval as a prospective adopter being terminated
- On the approved prospective adopter being approved as a foster parent in accordance with the Fostering Services Regulations
- If the approved prospective adopter gives written notice to the responsible authority that s/he no longer wishes to be temporarily approved as a foster parent in relation to C, with effect from 28 days

from the date on which the notice is received by the responsible authority or
- On C being placed for adoption with the approved prospective adopter in accordance with the Adoption and Children Act 2002 (as amended) [reg.25A(1)–(3)].

Independent Fostering Agencies – Discharge of Authority Functions [Reg.26 CPP&CR (England) Regulations 2010]

- An authority may make arrangements in accordance with reg.26 for the duties imposed on it by reg.14(3) (termination) and reg.22 (conditions to be complied with before placing a child with a local authority foster parent) to be discharged on its behalf by a registered person [reg.26(1)].

- No arrangements may be made under reg.26 unless the responsible authority has entered into a written agreement with the registered person which includes the information (reproduced below) set out in para.1 of Sch.5 of these regulations, and when the responsible authority proposes to make an arrangement under reg.26 in relation to a particular child, the written agreement must also include the matters set out in para.2 of Sch.5 [reg.26(2)].

- The responsible authority must report to the Chief Inspector of Education, Children's Services and Skills any concerns it may have about the services provided by a registered person [reg.26(3)].

Agreement with an Independent Fostering Agency (IFA) relating to the Discharge of the Responsible Authority's Functions [Sch.5 CPP&CR (England) Regulations 2010 in support of reg.26]

- The agreement must contain the following information:
    - Services to be provided to the responsible authority by the registered person
    - Arrangements for the selection by the responsible authority of F from those approved by the registered person
    - A requirement for the registered person to submit reports to the responsible authority on any placements as may be required by the responsible authority and

Care Planning, Placement & Case Review (England) Regulations 2010 (as amended)

- Arrangements for the termination of the agreement [Sch.5(1)].

■ If the agreement relates to a particular child, it must also contain the following information:

- F's details
- Details of any services that C is to receive and whether the services are to be provided by the responsible authority or by the registered provider
- Terms (including as to payment) of the proposed placement agreement
- Arrangements for record keeping about C and for the return of records at the end of the placement
- A requirement for the registered person to notify the responsible authority immediately in the event of concerns about the placement and
- Whether and on what basis other children may be placed with F [Sch.5(2)].

Provision for Different Types of Placement: Other Arrangements

General Duties of the Responsible Authority when Placing a Child in Other Arrangements [Reg.27 CPP&CR (England) Regulations 2010]

■ Before placing C in accommodation in an unregulated setting under s.22C(6)(d) ('other arrangements'), the responsible authority must:

- Be satisfied that the accommodation is suitable for C, having regard to the matters set out in Sch. 6 to these regulations (reproduced below)
- Unless it is not reasonably practicable arrange for C to visit the accommodation, and
- Inform the IRO.

Care Planning, Placement & Case Review (England) Regulations 2010 (as amended)

Matters to be Considered before Placing C in Accommodation in an Unregulated Setting under s.22C(6)(d) CA 1989 [Sch.6 CPP&CR (England) Regulations 2010 in support of reg.27]

- In respect of the accommodation:
  - Facilities and services provided
  - State of repair
  - Safety
  - Location
  - Support
  - Tenancy status
  - Financial commitment involved for C and their affordability [Sch.6 para.1].

- In respect of C, C's:
  - Views about the accommodation
  - Understanding of their rights and responsibilities in relation to the accommodation
  - Understanding of funding arrangements [Sch.6 para.2].

Visits by Responsible Authority's Representative etc

Frequency of Visits [Reg.28 CPP&CR (England) Regulations 2010]

- As part of its arrangements for supervising C's welfare, the responsible authority must ensure that its representative ('R') visits C wherever C is living in accordance with reg.28 [reg.28(1)].

- Subject to regs.28(3)–(6), the responsible authority must ensure that R visits C:
  - Within one week of the start of any placement
  - At intervals of not more than six weeks for the first year of any placement and thereafter

- If the placement is intended to last until C is 18, at intervals of not more than three months, and in any other case intervals of not more than six weeks [reg.28(2)].

■ When reg.19 applies, i.e. 'circumstances in which a child may be placed with P before assessment completed', the responsible authority must ensure that R visits C:

- At least once a week until the first review carried out in accordance with Part 6 and
- Thereafter at an interval of not more than six weeks [reg.28(3)].

■ If C is in a long term foster placement, has been in that placement for at least one year and is of sufficient age and understanding and agrees to be visited at intervals less than that required by reg.28(2) above, the responsible authority must ensure that R visits C at an interval of no more than six months [reg.28(3A) CPP&CR 2010 inserted by reg.5 Care Planning and Fostering (Miscellaneous Amendments) (England) Regulations 2015].

■ When reg.24 applies, i.e. 'temporary approval of relative, friend or other person connected with C', or an interim Care Order has been made in relation to C under s.38 and C is living with P, the responsible authority must ensure that R visits C:

- At least once a week until the first review carried out in accordance with Part 6
- Thereafter at intervals of not more than four weeks [reg.28(4)].

■ If a Care Order has been made in relation to C under s.31 (Care and Supervision Orders), and C is living with P, the responsible authority must ensure that R visits C:

- Within one week of the making of the Care Order
- Thereafter at intervals of not more than six weeks [s.28(5)].

■ If C is in the care of the responsible authority but another person is responsible for the arrangements under which C is living for the time being ('C's living arrangements'), the responsible authority must ensure that R visits C:

- Within one week of the start of C's living arrangements and within one week of any change to C's living arrangements
- At intervals of not more than six weeks for the first year thereafter
- At intervals of not more than three months in any subsequent year [reg.28(6)].

■ In addition to visits in accordance with reg.28(2)–(6), the responsible authority must ensure that R visits C:

- Whenever reasonably requested to do so by C; if C is provided with accommodation by the responsible authority, the appropriate person; or if C is in the care of the responsible authority but another person is responsible for her/his living arrangements, *that* person
- Within one week of first receiving notification under s.30A Care Standards Act 2000 (notification of matters relating to persons carrying on or managing certain establishments or agencies), when the children's home in which C is placed for the time being is referred to in the notification [reg.28(7)].

Conduct of Visit [Reg.29 CPP&CR (England) Regulations 2010]

■ On each visit, R must speak to C in private unless:

- C, being of sufficient age and understanding to do so, refuses
- R considers it inappropriate to do so, having regard to C's age and understanding, or
- R is unable to do so [reg.29].

Consequences of Visits [Reg.30 CPP&CR Regulations (England) 2010]

■ If, as a result of a visit carried out in accordance with the above regulations, R's assessment is that C's welfare is not adequately safeguarded and promoted by the placement, the responsible authority must review C's case in accordance with Part 6 [reg.30].

Care Planning, Placement & Case Review (England) Regulations 2010 (as amended)

Advice, Support & Assistance for the Child [Reg.31 CPP&CR (England) Regulations 2010]

- When making arrangements in accordance with s.23ZB(2)(b) for advice, support and assistance to be available to C between R's visits, the responsible authority must ensure that:

  - The arrangements are appropriate having regard to C's age and understanding, and give due consideration to C's religious persuasion, racial origin, cultural and linguistic background and to any disability C may have
  - So far as is reasonably practicable, having regard to C's age and understanding, C knows how to seek appropriate advice, support and assistance from them [reg.31].

Reviews of the Child's Case

General Duty of the Responsible Authority to Review the Child's Case [Reg.32 CPP&CR (England) Regulations 2010] and the Children's Homes and Looked after Children (Miscellaneous Amendments) (England) Regulations 2013

- The responsible authority must review C's case in accordance with these regulations [reg.32(1)].

- The responsible authority must not make any significant change to C's care plan unless the proposed change has first been considered at a review of C's case, unless this is not reasonably practicable [reg.32(2)].

- Nothing in these regulations prevents any review of C's case being carried out at the same time as any other review assessment or consideration of C's case under any other provision [reg.32(3)].

Care Planning, Placement & Case Review (England) Regulations 2010 (as amended)

Timing of Reviews [Reg.33 CPP&CR (England) Regulations 2010] and the Children's Homes and Looked After Children (Miscellaneous Amendments) (England) Regulations 2013

- The responsible authority must first review C's case within 20 working days of the date on which C becomes looked after [reg.33(1)].

- The second review must be carried out no more than three months after the first, and subsequent reviews must be carried out at intervals of no more than six months [reg.33(2)].

- The responsible authority must carry out a review *before* the time specified in reg.33(1) or (2) if:
  - The responsible authority considers that C is, or has been, persistently absent from a placement
  - The responsible authority is notified that the appropriate person (P), or the area authority is concerned that C is at risk of harm or that
  - C so requests it [reg.33(3)(aa)–(ac), but C's request is not required to be acceded to if the IRO considers that a review before standard reg.33 timings is not justified [reg.33(4) CPP&CR Regs.2010 as amended].
  - The IRO so requests
  - Reg.30 (consequences of R's report) applies
  - C is provided with accommodation under s.21(2)(b) or (c) (i.e. detained under PACE 1984, remanded or the subject of a Supervision Order with a residence requirement) and a review would not otherwise occur before C ceases to be so provided with accommodation
  - C is in the care of the authority and is detained in a secure training centre (STC), or a young offenders institution (YOI) and a review would not otherwise occur before C ceases to be so detained or
  - C is looked after but is *not* in the care of the responsible authority, the responsible authority propose to cease to provide accommodation for C, and accommodation will not subsequently be provided for C by C's parents or any person who is not C's parent but who has parental responsibility for C [reg.33(3)].

Care Planning, Placement & Case Review (England) Regulations 2010 (as amended)

Conduct of the Review [Reg.34 CPP&CR (England) Regulations 2010]

- The responsible authority must have a *policy* regarding the manner in which it will review C's case and provide a copy to C (unless not appropriate having regard to age and understanding), C's parents or any person who is not C's parent but who has parental responsibility for C, and any other person whose views the responsible authority consider to be relevant [reg.34(1);(2)].

- The considerations to which the responsible authority must have regard in reviewing each case are set out in Sch.7 to these regulations, reproduced below.

For Consideration at each Review [Sch.7 CPP&CR (England) Regulations 2010 in Support of Reg.35] as amended by Children's Homes and Looked After Children (Miscellaneous Amendments) (England) Regulations 2013

- The effect of any change in C's circumstances since the last review, in particular of any change made by the responsible authority to her/his care plan and whether decisions taken at the last review have been successfully implemented, and if not the reasons for that.

- Whether the responsible authority should seek any change in C's legal status.

- Whether there is a plan for permanence for C.

- The arrangements for contact and whether there is any need for changes to the arrangements in order to promote contact between C and P, or other connected persons.

- Whether C's placement continues to be the most appropriate available, having regard to the reports of R's visits to C, and whether any change to the placement plan or any other aspects of the arrangements made to provide C with accommodation is, or is likely to become necessary or desirable before the next review of C's case.

- Whether C's placement safeguards and promotes her/his welfare and whether any safeguarding concerns have been raised.

- C's educational needs, progress and development and whether any change to the arrangements for C's education and training is, or is likely to become, necessary or desirable to meet C's particular needs and to promote C's educational achievement before the next review of C's case, having regard to the advice of any person who provides C with education or training, in particular the designated teacher of any school at which C is a registered pupil.

- C's leisure interests.

- The report of the most recent assessment of C's state of health obtained in accordance with reg.8 and whether any change to the arrangements for C's health care is, or is likely to become, necessary or desirable before the next review of her/his case, having regard to the advice of any health care professional received since the date of that report, in particular C's registered medical practitioner.

- Whether C's needs related to C's identity are being met and whether any particular change is required, having regard to C's religious persuasion, racial origin and cultural background.

- Whether the arrangements made in accordance with reg.31 (advice, support and assistance for the child) continue to be appropriate and understood by C.

- Whether any arrangements need to be made for the time when C will no longer be looked after by the responsible authority.

- C's wishes and feelings, and the views of the IRO, about any aspect of the case and in particular about any changes the responsible authority has made since the last review or proposes to make to C's care plan.

- If reg.28(3) applies (visiting obligations if C is placed with P before reg.17 assessment completed), the frequency of R's visits.

- If C is a victim of trafficking or an UASC, whether his needs as a result of that status are being met [Sch.7 para.14 introduced by the Care Planning and Care Leavers (Amendment) Regulations 2014].

- Whether the delegation of authority to make decisions about C's care and upbringing, if any, recorded in her/his care plan by virtue of Sch. 2 para. 3(4A) continues to be appropriate and in C's best interests [Sch.7 para.15 introduced by Care Planning and Fostering (Miscellaneous Amendments) (England) Regulations 2015].

Role of the IRO [Reg.36 CPP&CR (England) Regulations 2010]

- The IRO *must*:
  - So far as reasonably practicable, attend any meeting held as part of the review ('the review meeting') and, if attending, chair it
  - Speak to C in private about the matters to be considered at the review unless C, being of sufficient understanding to do so, refuses or the IRO considers it inappropriate having regard to C's age and understanding
  - Ensure that so far as reasonably practicable, the wishes and feelings of C's parents or any person who is not C's parent but has parental responsibility for C and the views of the appropriate person have been ascertained and taken into account
  - Ensure the review is conducted in accordance with Part 6 and in particular that the persons responsible for implementing any decision taken in consequence of the review are identified, and that any failure to review the case in accordance with Part 6 or to take proper steps to implement decisions taken in consequence of the review are brought to the attention of an officer at an appropriate level of seniority within the responsible authority [reg.36(1)].

- The IRO *may*, if not satisfied that sufficient information has been provided by the responsible authority to enable proper consideration of any of the matters in Sch.7 (reproduced above), adjourn the review meeting once for not more than 20 working days, and no proposal considered in the course of the review may be implemented until the review has been completed [reg.36(2)].

Care Planning, Placement & Case Review (England) Regulations 2010 (as amended)

Arrangements for Implementing Decisions Arising out of Reviews [Reg.37 CPP&CR (England) Regulations 2010]

- The responsible authority must:
    - Make arrangements to implement decisions made in the course, or as a result, of the review, and
    - Inform the IRO of any significant failure to make such arrangements or any significant change of circumstances occurring after the review that affects those arrangements [reg.37].

Records of Reviews [Reg.38 CPP&CR (England) Regulations 2010]

- The responsible authority must ensure that a written report of the review is produced, and that the information obtained in the course of the review, details of proceedings at the review meeting, and any decisions made in the course of or as a result of the review are included in C's case record [reg.38].

Arrangements to be made when the Responsible Authority is Considering Ceasing to Look After a Child [Regs.39–44]

- When a responsible authority is considering ceasing to look after C, before making that decision it must:
    - Carry out an assessment of the suitability of the proposed arrangements for C's accommodation and maintenance when s/he ceases to be looked after by it
    - Carry out an assessment of the services and support that C, and if applicable P, might need when the responsible authority ceases to look after C
    - Ensure that C's wishes and feelings have been ascertained and given due consideration and

Care Planning, Placement & Case Review (England) Regulations 2010 (as amended)

- Consider whether, in all the circumstances and taking into account any services or support the responsible authority intend to provide, ceasing to look after C will safeguard and promote her/his welfare [reg.39(1);(2) as substituted by reg.7 Care Planning and Fostering (Miscellaneous Amendments) (England) Regulations 2015].

- The responsible authority must include in C's care plan (or if reg.47B(4) applies, the detention placement plan), details of the advice, assistance and support that the responsible authority intends to provide for C when s/he ceases to be looked after by it [reg.39(3) as substituted by reg.7 Care Planning and Fostering (Miscellaneous Amendments) (England) Regulations 2015].

- Subject to reg.39(5), if C has been a looked after child for at least 20 working days, any decision to cease to look after her/him must not be put into effect until approved by a nominated officer [reg.39(4) as substituted by reg.7 Care Planning and Fostering (Miscellaneous Amendments) (England) Regulations 2015].

- In any case where C is 16 or 17 and not in the care of the local authority, the decision to cease to look after her/him must not be put into effect until approved by the responsible authority's DCS [reg.39(5) as substituted by reg.7 Care Planning and Fostering (Miscellaneous Amendments) (England) Regulations 2015].

- Before approving a decision under either of the above two provisions, the nominated officer/DCS must be satisfied that:
  - The requirements of reg.9(1)(b)(i) have been complied with
  - Ceasing to look after C will safeguard and promote her/his welfare
  - The support the responsible authority intend to provide will safeguard and promote her/his welfare
  - C's relatives have been consulted, where appropriate
  - The IRO has been consulted and
  - When appropriate, regulations 40–43 described below have been complied with [reg.39(6) as substituted by reg.7 Care Planning and Fostering (Miscellaneous Amendments) (England) Regulations 2015].

Care Planning, Placement & Case Review (England) Regulations 2010 (as amended)

Eligible Child: Meaning [Reg.40 CPP&CR Regulations 2010]

- For the purposes of para.19B(2)(b) of Sch.2 CA 1989 (which defines an 'eligible' child), the 'prescribed period' is 13 weeks and the 'prescribed age' is 14 [reg.40(1)].

- If, though, C is a child to whom reg.48 (short breaks) applies, C is *not* an eligible child despite falling within para.19B(2) of Schedule 2 [reg.40(2)].

Eligible Child: General Duties [Reg.41 CPP&CR Regulations 2010]

- If C *is* an eligible child, the responsible authority:
  - Must assess her/his needs in accordance with reg.42 and
  - Prepare C's pathway plan, in accordance with reg.43 [reg.41].

Eligible Child: Assessment of Needs [Reg.42 CPP&CR Regulations 2010]

- The responsible authority must complete the assessment of C's needs in accordance with para.19B(4) of Sch.2 CA 1989 not more than three months after the date on which s/he reaches the age of 16 or becomes an eligible child after that age [reg.42(1)].

- In carrying out its assessment of C's likely needs when it ceases to look after her/him, the responsible authority must take account of the following considerations:
  - C's state of health (including physical, emotional and mental health) and development
  - C's continuing need for education, training or employment
  - The support that will be available to C from C's parents and other connected persons
  - C's actual and anticipated financial resources and capacity to manage personal finances independently
  - The extent to which C possesses the practical and other skills necessary for independent living
  - C's continuing needs for care, support and accommodation

- The wishes and feelings of C, any parent of C's and any person who is not C's parent but who has parental responsibility for C and the 'appropriate person'
- The views of any person or educational institution that provides C with education or training (and if C has a statement of special educational needs, the local authority that maintains the statement), the IRO, any person providing health (physical, mental or emotional health) or dental care or treatment to C, the personal adviser appointed for C, and any other person whose views the responsible authority or C consider may be relevant
- Where C has been a victim of trafficking or is an UASC, any needs that C has as a result [reg.4 Care Planning and Care Leavers (Amendment) Regulations 2014.

Eligible Child: Pathway Plan [Reg.43 & Sch.8 CPP&CR Regulations 2010]

■ A *pathway plan* must be prepared as soon as possible after the assessment of C's needs and must include, in particular, C's care plan and the following information referred to in Sch.8 of these regulations:

- Name of C's personal adviser (PA)
- Nature and level of contact and personal support to be provided to C, and by whom
- Details of the accommodation C is to occupy when C ceases to be looked after
- Plan for C's continuing education or training when C ceases to be looked after
- How the responsible authority will assist C in obtaining employment or other purposeful activity or occupation
- Support to be provided to enable C to develop and sustain appropriate family and social relationships
- A programme to develop the practical and other skills C needs to live independently
- Financial support to be provided to enable C to meet her/his accommodation and maintenance costs

- C's health care needs, including any physical, emotional or mental health needs and how they are to be met when C ceases to be looked after
- Responsible authority's contingency plans for action to be taken in the event that the pathway plan ceases to be effective for any reason [reg.43(1) & Sch.8].

■ The pathway plan must, in relation to each of the matters referred to in Sch.8 above, set out the:

- Manner in which the responsible authority proposes to meet C's needs, and
- Date by which, and by whom, any action required to implement any aspect of the plan will be carried out [reg.43(2)].

Eligible Child: Functions of the Personal Adviser [Reg.44 CPP&CR Regulations 2010]

■ The personal adviser's functions in relation to C are to:

- Provide advice (including practical advice) and support
- Participate in reviews of C's case carried out under Part 6
- Liaise with the responsible authority in the implementation of the pathway plan
- Co-ordinate the provision of services and to take reasonable steps to ensure C makes use of such services
- Remain informed about C's progress and wellbeing
- Maintain a written record of contacts with C [reg.44].

Independent Reviewing Officers & Independent Visitors [Regs.45–47]

Additional Functions of Independent Reviewing Officers [Reg.45 CPP&CR (England) Regulations 2010]

- The IRO must ensure that, having regard to C's age and understanding, C has been informed by the responsible authority of the steps s/he may take under the 1989 Act and in particular, when appropriate:

  - C's right to apply, with leave, for a s.8 CA 1989 order and, if C is in the care of the responsible authority, to apply for the discharge of the care order, and
  - The availability of the procedure established under s.26(3)(a) CA 1989 for considering any representations (including complaints) C may wish to make about the discharge by the responsible authority of its functions, including the availability of assistance to make such representations under s.26A(b) (advocacy services) [reg.45(1)].

- If C wishes to take legal proceedings under the 1989 Act, the IRO must:

  - Establish whether an appropriate adult is able and willing to assist C to obtain legal advice or bring proceedings on C's behalf, and
  - If there is no such person, assist C to obtain such advice [reg.45(2)].

- The IRO must consider whether it would be appropriate to refer C's case to an officer of the Children and Family Court Advisory and Support Service (Cafcass) if

  - In the opinion of the IRO, the responsible authority has failed in any significant respect to make C's care plan in accordance with these regulations, review C's case in accordance with them, or to implement effectively any decision taken in consequence of a review, or is otherwise in breach of its duties to C in any material respect, and
  - Having drawn the failure to the attention of persons at an appropriate level of seniority within the responsible authority, it has

not been addressed to the satisfaction of the IRO within a reasonable period of time [reg.45(3)].

■ When consulted by the responsible authority about any matter concerning C, or when informed of any matter relating to C in accordance with these regulations, the IRO must:

- Ensure that the responsible authority has ascertained, and given due consideration to, C's wishes and feelings concerning the matter in question, and
- Consider whether to request a review of C's case [reg.45(4)].

Qualifications & Experience of Independent Reviewing Officers [Reg.46 CPP&CR (England) Regulations 2010]

■ The IRO must be registered as a social worker in a register maintained by the Health & Care Professions Council (HCPC) or by the Care Council for Wales under s.56 Care Standards Act 2000 or in a corresponding register maintained under the law of Scotland or Northern Ireland [reg.46(1)].

■ The IRO must have sufficient relevant social work experience with children and families to perform the functions of an IRO set out in s.25B(1) and under these regulations in an independent manner and having regard to C's best interests [reg.46(2)].

■ The responsible authority must *not* appoint any of the following as the IRO:

- A person involved in preparing C's care plan or the management of C's case
- R (the local authority representative who visits C in accordance with arrangements made under s.23ZA)
- C's personal adviser
- A person with management responsibilities in relation to any of the above three persons
- A person with control over the resources allocated to the case [reg.46(3)].

Care Planning, Placement & Case Review (England) Regulations 2010 (as amended)

Independent Visitors [Reg.47 CPP&CR (England) Regulations 2010]

- A person appointed by the responsible authority as an independent visitor under s.23ZB(1) is to be regarded as independent of that authority when the person appointed is not connected with the responsible authority by virtue of being:
    - A member of the responsible authority or any of its committees or sub-committees, whether elected or co-opted
    - An officer of the responsible authority employed in the exercise of the functions referred to in s.18(2) Children Act 2004 or
    - A spouse, civil partner or other person (whether of different or same sex) living in the same household as the partner of, a person falling within either of the two categories above [reg.47].

Miscellaneous [Regs.48–51]

Application of these Regulations with Modifications to Short Breaks [Reg.48 CPP&CR Regulations (England) 2010]

- In the circumstances set out in para.2, these regulations apply with the modifications set out in para.3[reg.48(1)].
- The circumstances are that:
    - C is *not* in the care of the responsible authority
    - The responsible authority has arranged to place C in a series of short-term placements with the same person or at the same place ('short breaks'), and
    - The arrangement is such that no single placement is intended to last for more than 17 days; at the end of each such placement C returns to the care of either C's parent or a person who is not C's parent but who has parental responsibility for C and the short breaks do not exceed 75 days in total in any period of 12 months [reg.48(2)].
- The modifications are that:

- Reg.5 (preparation and content of the care plan) and reg.9 (placement plan) do *not* apply but instead the care plan must set out the arrangements that have been made to meet C's needs, with particular regard to her/his health and emotional and behavioural development, in particular in relation to any disability C may have; promoting contact between C and C's parents and any other person who is not C's parent but who has parental responsibility for C during any period when C is placed; C's leisure interests and promoting C's educational achievement *and* must include the information set out in paras.3 and 4 of Sch.2 to these regulations, as appropriate
- Reg.7 (health care), reg.13 (notification of placements) and reg.49(2)(b) (case record as per reg.7) do not apply
- Reg.28(2) (frequency of visits by a representative of the responsible authority) does not apply, but instead the responsible authority must ensure its representative visits C on a day when s/he is in fact placed, at regular intervals to be agreed with the IRO and C's parents (or any person who is not C's parent but who has parental responsibility for C), and recorded in the care plan before the start of the first placement, and in any event the first visit must take place within three months of the start of the placement or as soon as practicable thereafter and subsequent visits at intervals of not more than six months for as long as the short breaks continue
- Reg.33 (timing of reviews) does not apply, but instead the responsible authority must first review C's case within three months of the beginning of the first placement, and the second and subsequent reviews must be carried out at intervals of no more than six months thereafter [reg.48(3)].

Records: Establishment [Reg.49 CPP&CR Regulations (England) 2010]

- The responsible authority must establish and maintain a written case record for C, if one is not already in existence [reg.49(1)].
- The record must include:
  - C's care plan, including any changes made to the care plan and any subsequent plans

- Reports obtained under reg.7 (health care)
- Any other document created or considered as part of any assessment of C's needs or of any review of C's case
- Any court order relating to C
- Details of any arrangements that have been made by the responsible authority with any other local authority or with an independent fostering agency (IFA) under reg.26 and Sch.5 or with a provider of social work services under which any of the responsible authority's functions in relation to C are discharged by that local authority or IFA or provider of social work services, details of those arrangements [reg.49(2)].

Records: Retention & Confidentiality [Reg.50 CPP&CR Regulations (England) 2010]

■ The responsible authority must retain the case record relating to C either:

- Until the 75th anniversary of C's birth, or
- If C dies before attaining the age of 18, for 15 years beginning with the date of C's death [reg.50(1)].

■ The responsible authority must secure the safe keeping of C's case record and take any necessary steps to ensure that information contained in it is treated as confidential, subject only to any:

- Provision of, or made under or by virtue of, a statute under which access to such records or information may be obtained or given
- Court order under which access to such records or information may be obtained or given [reg.50(2)].

Records: Children Placed in an 'Area Authority'

■ Statutory guidance (Volume 2) indicates that an Area Authority should maintain a list of all the notifications of looked after children placed in its area so that it can fulfil its statutory duties under the CA 1989.

FOSTERING SERVICES (ENGLAND) REGULATIONS 2011 (AS AMENDED)

Fostering Services (England) Regulations 2011 (as amended)

Statement of Purpose & Children's Guide [Regs.1–4]

Statement of Purpose & Children's Guide [Regs.3 & 4 Fostering Services (England) Regulations 2011]

- The fostering service provider must compile a written 'statement of purpose' which includes:

  - The aims and objectives of the fostering service
  - A statement as to the facilities and services (including any parent and child arrangements) to be provided by the fostering service [reg.3(1)].

- The fostering service provider must provide a copy of that statement to the Chief Inspector, place a copy on its website (if it has one) and make a copy of it available upon request to:

  - Any person working for the purpose of the fostering service
  - Any foster parent or prospective foster parent of the service
  - Any child placed with a foster parent by the fostering service and
  - The parent of any such child [reg.3(2)].

- The fostering service provider must also produce a 'children's guide' which includes:

  - A summary of the statement of purpose
  - A summary of the organisation's representation and complaints procedure as specified for IFAs (under reg.18(1)), and for local authorities and voluntary organisations (s.26(3) and (s.59(4)(b) CA 1989 respectively
  - Postal and email address and telephone number of the Chief Inspector [reg.3(3)].

- The fostering service provider must provide copies of the children's guide to:

  - The Chief Inspector
  - Each foster parent approved by the fostering service provider and

Fostering Services (England) Regulations 2011 (as amended)

- (Subject to age and understanding) each child placed by it [reg.3(4)].

■ Subject to the appointment of a manager, the fostering service provider must ensure that its fostering service is at all times conducted in a manner which is consistent with its statement of purpose [reg.3(5)].

NB. Nothing in reg.3(5) requires or authorises the fostering service provider to contravene or fail to comply with any other provision of these regulations or, in the case of an IFA, any conditions for the time being in force in relation to the registration of the registered person under Part 2 CSA 2000 [reg.3(6)].

■ The fostering service provider must:

- Keep under review and where appropriate, revise the statement of purpose and children's guide
- Notify the Chief Inspector within 28 days of any such revision and
- If the children's guide is revised, supply a copy to each foster parent approved by the service provider and (subject to age and understanding), to each child placed by it [reg.4].

Management of Fostering Service [Regs.5–10]

Fostering Agency: Fitness of Provider [Reg.5 & Sch. 1 Fostering Services (England) Regulations 2011]

■ A person must not carry on a fostering agency unless s/he satisfies the requirements of reg.5(2) as follows:

- In the case of an individual carrying on an IFA otherwise than in partnership with others, that person
- In the case of an individual carrying on an IFA in partnership with others, that person and each of the other partners
- In the case of a partnership carrying on an IFA, each of the partners
- In the case of an organisation carrying on an IFA, where it has given notice to the Chief Inspector of the name, address and position in the

Fostering Services (England) Regulations 2011 (as amended)

organisation of an individual ('the responsible individual') who is a director, manager, secretary or other officer of the organisation and is responsible for supervising the management of the IFA, the responsible individual [reg.5(1)].

■ The requirements are that:

- The person is of integrity and good character
- The person is physically and mentally fit to carry on the fostering agency and
- Full and satisfactory information is available in relation to the person in respect of each of the matters specified in Sch.1 [reg.5(2)].

■ The required information of Sch.1 is:

- Positive proof of identity, including a recent photograph
- *Either* where the certificate is required for a purpose relating to Part 2 of the 2000 Act, or the position falls within reg.5A Police Act 1997 (Criminal Records) Regulations 2002, an enhanced criminal record certificate issued under s.113B of the Police Act 1997 which includes suitability information relating to children (within the meaning of s.113BA(2) of that Act) or
- In any other case, a standard criminal record certificate issued under s.113A Police Act 1997
- Two written references, including a reference from the person's most recent employer, if any
- Where a person has previously worked in a position whose duties involved work with children or vulnerable adults, so far as reasonably practicable verification of the reason why the employment or position ended
- Documentary evidence of any relevant qualification
- A full employment history, together with a satisfactory written explanation of any gaps in employment.

■ A person is not allowed to carry on a fostering agency if s/he has:

- Been adjudged bankrupt or sequestration of her/his estate has been awarded and (in either case) s/he has not been discharged and the bankruptcy order has not been annulled or rescinded or a moratorium

Fostering Services (England) Regulations 2011 (as amended)

period under a debt relief order within the meaning of s.251A Insolvency Act 1986 applies in relation to her/him or
- Made a composition or arrangement with creditors in respect of which s/he has not been discharged [reg.5(3)].

Fostering Agency: Appointment of Manager [Reg.6 Fostering Services (England) Regulations 2011]

- The registered provider must appoint an individual to manage the fostering agency [reg.6(1)].

- If the registered provider is an organisation, it must not appoint the person who is the responsible individual as the manager, or if the registered provider is a partnership, it must not appoint any of the partners as the manager [reg.6(2)].

- The registered provider must, without delay, notify the Chief Inspector of the:
  - Name of the person appointed in accordance with this regulation and
  - Date on which the appointment is to take effect [reg.6(3)].

Fostering Agency: Fitness of Manager [Reg.7 Fostering Services (England) Regulations 2011]

- A person must not manage a fostering agency unless s/he is fit to do so [reg.7(1)].

- A person is not fit to manage a fostering agency unless:
  - S/he is of integrity and good character
  - Having regard to the agency's size, statement of purpose and numbers and needs of children placed by it, s/he has the qualifications, skills and experience necessary for managing the agency and is physically and mentally fit for the role
  - Full and satisfactory information is available in relation to her/him as detailed in Sch.1 Fostering Services (England) Regulations 2011 outlined above under reg.5 [reg.7.(2)].

Fostering Services (England) Regulations 2011 (as amended)

Fostering Agency: Registered Person – General Requirements [Reg.8 Fostering Services (England) Regulations 2011]

- The registered provider and registered manager must, having regard to the agency's size, statement of purpose, and number and needs of children placed by it, the need to safeguard and promote children placed, carry on/manage the fostering agency with sufficient care, competence and skill [reg.8(1)].

- The registered provider must ensure that the following undertake, from time to time, such training as is appropriate to ensure they have the experience and skills necessary for carrying on the agency:
  - If the registered provider is an individual, that person
  - If the registered person is an organisation, the responsible individual
  - If the registered provider is a partnership, one of the partners [reg.8(2)].

- The registered manager must also undertake from time to time such training as is appropriate to ensure s/he has the experience and skills necessary for managing the fostering agency [reg.8(3)].

Notification of Offences [Reg.9 Fostering Services (England) Regulations 2011]

- If the registered person or the responsible individual is convicted of any criminal offence in England or Wales or elsewhere, s/he must immediately give notice to the Chief Inspector of the:
  - Date and place of the conviction
  - Offence of which s/he was convicted
  - Penalty imposed [reg.9].

Local Authority Fostering Service: Manager [Reg.10 Fostering Services (England) Regulations 2011]

- Each local authority must appoint one of its officers to manage its fostering services and must without delay notify the Chief Inspector of the name of the appointee and the date on which the appointment is to take effect [reg.10(1)].

- The requirements in regs.7, 8 and 9 (fitness of manger, general requirements of registered person and notification of offences) are applicable to the manager of a local authority fostering service as well as to the manager of a fostering agency in relation to that agency [reg.10(2)].

- The local authority must without delay notify the Chief Inspector if the fostering services manager appointed under reg.10(1) ceases to manage that service [reg.10(3)].

    NB. Volume 4 (para.4.9) confirms that a motoring offence dealt with by way of a fixed penalty notice does not need to be notified to Ofsted, e.g. someone failing to wear a seatbelt, paying her/his fine and thus not being prosecuted so that there will be no record of the offence.

Conduct of Fostering Service [Regs.11–22 Fostering Services (England) Regulations 2011]

Independent Fostering Agencies: Duty to Secure Welfare [Reg.11 Fostering Services (England) Regulations 2011]

- The registered person in respect of an independent fostering agency must ensure that:
    - The welfare of children placed or to be placed with foster parents is safeguarded and promoted at all times
    - Before making any decisions affecting a child placed or to be placed, due consideration is given to the child's wishes and feelings having regard to her/his age and understanding, religious persuasion, racial origin and cultural and linguistic background [reg.11].

    NB. A voluntary organisation which places children with foster parents under s.59(1) CA 1989 has similar duties under s.61 to a local authority under s.22 of that Act.

Fostering Services (England) Regulations 2011 (as amended)

Arrangements for the Protection of Children [Reg.12 Fostering Services (England) Regulations 2011]

- The fostering service provider must prepare and implement a written policy which:
  - Is intended to safeguard children placed with foster parents, from abuse or neglect and
  - Sets out the procedure to be followed in the event of any allegation of abuse or neglect [reg.12(1)].

- The written policy must include a statement of measures to be taken to safeguard children placed with foster parents before making parent and child arrangements with that foster parent [reg.12(2)].

- The allegation of abuse/neglect procedure must provide in particular for:
  - Liaison and co-operation with any local authority which is, or may be, making 'child protection enquiries' (and for this regulation that means under *any* provision of the CA 1989) in relation to any child placed by the fostering service provider
  - Prompt referral to the area authority of any allegation of abuse or neglect affecting any child placed by the fostering service provider
  - Notification of instigation and outcome of any such enquiries involving a child placed by the fostering service provider, to the Chief Inspector
  - Written records to be kept of any allegation of abuse or neglect, and of action taken in response
  - Consideration to be given to the measures which may be necessary to protect children placed with foster parents following an allegation of abuse or neglect
  - Arrangements to be made for persons working for purpose of a fostering service, foster parents and children placed by the service, to have access to information which would enable them to contact the area authority and the Chief Inspector regarding any concern about child welfare or safety [reg.12(3);(5)].

NB. The first and third of the above bullets and reference to the area authority in the final bullet do not apply to a local authority fostering service [reg.12(4)].

Behaviour Management & Children Missing from Foster Parent's Home [Reg.13 Fostering Services (England) Regulations 2011]

- The fostering service provider must prepare and implement a written policy on acceptable measures of control, restraint and discipline of children placed with foster parents [reg.13(1)].

- The fostering service provider must take all reasonable steps to ensure that:
  - No form of corporal punishment is used on any child placed with a foster parent
  - No child placed with foster parents is subject to any measure of control, restraint or discipline which is excessive or unreasonable and
  - Physical restraint is used on a child only when it is necessary to prevent likely injury to the child or other persons or likely serious damage to property [reg.13(2)].

- The fostering service provider must prepare and implement a policy, which is agreed with the local police, setting out the:
  - Measures to be followed to prevent children placed with foster carers from going missing from their placement
  - Procedure to be followed when a child is missing from a foster carer's home without permission [reg.13(3) Fostering Services (England) Regulations as substituted by reg.28 Children's Homes and Looked After Children (Miscellaneous Amendments) (England) Regulations 2013].

Duty to Promote Contact [Reg.14 Fostering Services (England) Regulations 2011]

- The fostering service provider must, subject to the provisions of the care plan and any court order relating to contact, promote contact between a child placed with a foster parent and the child's parents, relatives and friends, unless such contact is not reasonably practicable or consistent with the child's welfare.

Health of Children Placed With Foster Parents [Reg.15 Fostering Services (England) Regulations 2011]

- ■ The service provider must promote the health and development of children placed with carers and in particular ensure that each child:

  - Is a registered patient with a general medical practitioner who provides primary medical services under Part 4 National Health Services Act 2006
  - Has access to such medical, dental, nursing, psychological and psychiatric advice, treatment and other services as s/he may require
  - Is provided with such individual support, aids and equipment as s/he may require as a result of any particular health needs or disability
  - Is provided with guidance, support and advice on health and personal care and health promotion issues appropriate to needs and wishes.

NB. In reg.15, 'general medical practitioner' means a medical practitioner whose name is included in the General Practitioner Register kept by the General Medical Council under s.34C Medical Act 1983 [reg.15(3)].

Education, Employment & Leisure Activities [Reg.16 Fostering Services (England) Regulations 2011]

- ■ The service provider must promote the educational attainment of children who are placed with foster parents [reg.16(1)].

- ■ In particular, the service provider must:

  - Implement a procedure for monitoring the educational attainment, progress and school attendance of children placed with foster parents
  - Promote the regular school attendance and participation in school activities of children of compulsory school age placed with foster parents and
  - Provide foster parents with such information and assistance, including equipment, as may be necessary to meet the educational needs of children placed with them [reg.16(2)].

Fostering Services (England) Regulations 2011 (as amended)

- The service provider must ensure any education it provides for any child placed with foster parents who is of compulsory school age but not attending is efficient and suitable to the child's age, ability, aptitude, and any special educational needs s/he may have [reg.16(3)].

- The fostering service provider must ensure that foster parents promote the leisure interests of children placed with them [reg.16(4)].

- When any child placed with foster parents is above compulsory school age, the fostering service provider must assist with making and implementing arrangements for the young person's education, training and employment [reg.16(5)].

Support, Training & Information for Foster Parents [Reg.17 Fostering Services (England) Regulations 2011]

- The fostering service provider must provide foster parents with such training, advice, information and support (including support out of office hours) as appears necessary in the interests of children placed with them [reg.17(1)].

- The fostering service provider must take all reasonable steps to ensure that foster parents are familiar with and act in accordance with the policies established about child protection (reg.12(1)), behaviour management (reg.13(1)) and being missing without permission from a foster parent's home (reg.13(3)) [reg.17(2)].

- The fostering service provider must ensure that, in relation to any child placed or to be placed with a foster parent, the foster parent is given information, which is kept up to date as to enable her/him to provide appropriate care for the child, and in particular that each foster parent is provided with a copy of the most recent version of the child's care plan provided to the fostering service provider under reg.6(3)(d) Care Planning, Placements and Case Review (England) Regulations [reg.17(3)].

Fostering Services (England) Regulations 2011 (as amended)

Independent Fostering Agencies: Complaints & Representations
[Reg.18 Fostering Services (England) Regulations 2011]

- Subject to para.7, the registered person of an independent fostering agency must establish a written procedure for considering complaints made by or on behalf of children placed by the agency and foster parents approved by the agency [reg.18(1)].

- The procedure must in particular provide:
  - For an opportunity for informal resolution of the complaint at an early stage
  - That no person subject of a complaint takes any part in its consideration other than if the registered person considers it appropriate, at the informal resolution stage only
  - For dealing with complaints about the registered person
  - For complaints to be made by a person acting on behalf of a child
  - For arrangements for the procedure to be made known to placed children, parents, and persons working for the purposes of the independent fostering agency [reg.18(2)].

- A copy of the procedure must be supplied on request to any of the above individuals and must include:
  - Name, address (including email address) and phone number of the Chief Inspector and
  - Details of procedure (if any) notified to the registered person by the Chief Inspector for making complaints to it about the agency [reg.18(3)].

- The registered person must ensure that a record is made of any complaint, the action taken in response and the outcome of the investigation [reg.18(4)].

- The registered person must ensure that:
  - Children are enabled to make a complaint or representation and
  - No child is subject to any reprisal for making a complaint or representation [reg.18(5)].

- The registered person must supply the Chief Inspector with an annual summary of complaints made in the preceding 12 months and the action taken in response [reg.18(6)].

    NB. Reg.18 apart from para. 5 (record of complaints) does not apply in relation to any matter to which the CA 1989 Representations Procedure (England) Regulations 2006 applies [reg.18(7)].

Staffing of Fostering Service [Reg.19 Fostering Services (England) Regulations 2011]

- The fostering service provider must ensure that there is at all times a sufficient number of suitably qualified, competent and experienced persons working for the purposes of the fostering service, having regard to the:
    - Size of the service, its statement of purpose and the number and needs of the children placed by it
    - Need to safeguard and promote the health and welfare of children placed with foster parents.

Fitness of Workers [Reg.20 Fostering Services (England) Regulations 2011]

- The fostering service provider must not:
    - Employ a person to work for the purposes of the fostering service unless s/he is fit to work for the purposes of the fostering service
    - Allow a person who is employed by someone other than the registered person to work in the service in a position in which s/he may in the course of her/his duties have regular contact with children placed by the service [reg.20(1);(2)].

- A person is not 'fit' to work for the purposes of a fostering service unless:
    - S/he is of integrity and good character
    - S/he has the qualifications, skills and experience necessary for the work s/he is to perform
    - S/he is physically and mentally fit for the purposes of the work to be performed and

- Full and satisfactory information is available about her/him as per Sch. 1 [reg.20(3)] (see pages 73–74 for a summary of Sch.1 requirements).

■ The service provider must also take reasonable steps to ensure non-employees who have less than regular contact with children placed as per reg.20(2) are appropriately supervised [reg.20(4)].

Employment of Staff [Reg.21 Fostering Services (England) Regulations 2011]

■ The fostering service provider must:

- Ensure all permanent appointments are subject to satisfactory completion of a probation period
- Provide all employees with a job description [reg.21(1)].

■ The fostering service provider must operate a disciplinary procedure which, in particular:

- Provides for the suspension of an employee where necessary in the interests of the safety or welfare of children placed with foster parents
- Provides that failure on the part of an employee to report to an appropriate person an incident of abuse, or suspected abuse, of a child placed with foster parents is a ground on which disciplinary proceedings may be instituted [reg.21(2)].

■ An appropriate person for the above purpose is:

- In any case, the registered person/manager of a local authority fostering service, an officer of the Chief Inspector, an officer of the responsible authority or (if applicable) the area authority, a police officer or an officer of the NSPCC
- For an employee of an independent fostering agency, an officer of the placing authority and
- For an employee of a fostering agency, an officer of the local authority in whose area the agency is situated [reg.21(3)].

■ The fostering service provider must ensure that all persons employed by her/him:

Fostering Services (England) Regulations 2011 (as amended)

- Receive appropriate training, supervision and appraisal and
- Are enabled from time to time to obtain further qualifications appropriate to the work they perform [reg.21(4)].

Records with Respect to Fostering Services [Reg.22 & Sch. 2 Fostering Services (England) Regulations 2011]

- ■ The fostering service provider must maintain and keep up to date (as per Sch.2 reproduced below) a register which records, with respect to each child placed with a foster parent:

  - Date of her/his placement
  - Name and address of her/his foster parent
  - Date on which s/he ceased to be placed there
  - Address prior to the placement
  - Address on leaving the placement
  - Child's placing authority (if it is not the fostering service provider)
  - The statutory provision under which s/he was placed with foster parents.

- ■ The fostering service provider must also maintain and keep up to date a record showing in respect of each person working for the fostering service provider:

  - Her/his full name
  - Her/his sex
  - Date of birth
  - Home address
  - Qualifications relevant to and experience of work involving children
  - Whether employed by the provider under a contract of service or a contract for services, or is employed by someone other than the fostering service provider and
  - Whether s/he works full or part-time and if part-time, the average number of hours worked per week [Sch.2 para.2].

- ■ The fostering service provider must also maintain a record of all accidents occurring to children whilst placed with foster parents [Sch.2 para. 3].

NB. All the above records must be retained for a period of 15 years from the date of the last entry [reg.22(2)].

Approval of Foster Parents [Regs.23–32 Fostering Services (England) Regulations 2011]

Constitution & Membership of Fostering Panel [Reg.23 Fostering Services (England) Regulations 2011]

- The fostering service provider must maintain a list of persons who are considered by them to be suitable to be members of a fostering panel ('the central list'), including one or more social workers who have at least three years' relevant post-qualifying experience [reg.23(1)].

   NB. There is no limit to the number of people who may be included on the central list [Volume 4 para. 5.4].

- A person who is included on the central list may at any time ask to be removed from the central list by giving one month's notice in writing [reg.23(2)].

- When the fostering service provider is of the opinion that a person included on the central list is unsuitable or unable to remain on the list, the fostering service provider may remove that person's name from the list by giving her/him one month's notice in writing [reg.23(3)].

- Subject to reg.23(5), the fostering service provider must constitute one or more fostering panels, as necessary, to perform the functions of a fostering panel under these regulations, and must appoint panel members including, from persons on the central list:

    - A person to chair the panel who, in the case of any appointment made after 01.10.11, must be independent of the fostering service provider, and

Fostering Services (England) Regulations 2011 (as amended)

- One or two persons who may act as chair if the person appointed to chair the panel is absent or that office is vacant ('the vice chairs') [reg.23(4)].

NB. Volume 4 para. 5.12 confirms that there is no requirement for a vice chair to be independent of the fostering service, though this would be 'preferable where feasible'; that it is allowable to have more than two vice chairs and that there is no maximum or minimum tenure for members.

- A fostering panel may be constituted jointly by any two or more fostering service providers, in which case the appointment of members must be made by agreement between the fostering service providers [reg.23(5)].

- A local authority may pay to any member of a fostering panel constituted by them such fee as they may determine, being a fee of a reasonable amount [reg.23(6)].

- The fostering service provider must ensure that the fostering panel has sufficient members, and that individual members have between them the experience and expertise necessary to effectively discharge the functions of the panel [reg.23(7)].

- Any fostering panel member may resign at any time by giving one month's notice in writing to the fostering service provider which appointed her/him [reg.23(8)].

- When a fostering service provider is of the opinion that any member of the fostering panel appointed by it is unsuitable or unable to continue as a panel member, it may terminate that member's appointment at any time by giving the member notice in writing [reg.23(9)].

- For the purposes of this reg.23 and reg.24:

  - A person is not independent of the fostering service provider if s/he is currently approved by the fostering service provider as a foster parent
  - In the case of a local authority fostering service, the person is an elected member of that local authority, or is employed by that local authority for the purposes of the fostering service or for the purposes

of any of that local authority's functions relating to the protection or placement of children, or
- In the case of a fostering agency, the person is employed by, or is a trustee of, that fostering agency and
- A 'social worker' means a person who is registered as a social worker in a register maintained by the HCPC or by the Care Council for Wales under s.56 Care Standards Act 2000 (as amended) or in a corresponding register maintained under the law of Scotland or Northern Ireland [reg.23(10)].

NB. Volume 4 paras. 5.4–5.6 confirm that there is no requirement for a panel to have a fixed membership, though a 'core' membership may be helpful. Numbers at a panel should not be so large as to make it difficult to chair the meeting or to intimidate prospective foster carers or anyone else attending the meeting.

Meetings of Fostering Panel [Reg.24 Fostering Services (England) Regulations 2011]

- No business may be conducted by a fostering panel unless at least the following meet as the panel:

  - Either the person appointed to chair the panel or one of the vice chairs
  - One member who is a social worker who has at least three years' relevant post-qualifying experience, and
  - Three, or in the case of a fostering panel established under reg.23(5), four other members, *and*
  - If the chairperson is not present and the vice chairperson who is present is not independent of the fostering service provider, at least one of the other panel members must be independent of the fostering service provider [reg.24(1)].

- A fostering panel must make a written record of its proceedings and the reasons for its recommendations [reg.24(2)].

Fostering Services (England) Regulations 2011 (as amended)

Functions of Fostering Panel [Reg.25 Fostering Services (England) Regulations 2011]

- The functions of the fostering panel in respect of cases referred to it by the service provider are:

  - To consider each application for approval and to recommend whether or not a person is suitable to be a foster parent
  - When it recommends approval, to recommend the terms on which the approval is to be given
  - To recommend whether a person remains suitable to act as a foster parent, and whether the terms of her/his approval remain appropriate – on the first routine review as per reg.28(2) and on the occasion of any other review if requested to do so by the fostering service provider as per reg.28(5) or reg.28(10)
  - To consider any case referred to it under reg.27(9) or reg.28(10) [reg.25(1)].

- In considering what recommendation to make under reg.25(1) above, the fostering panel:

  - Must consider and take into account all of the information passed to it in accordance with regs.26, 27 or 28 as the case may be
  - May request the fostering service provider to obtain any other relevant information which the fostering panel considers necessary or to provide such other assistance as the fostering panel may request and
  - May obtain such legal advice or medical advice it considers necessary [reg.25(2)].

- In relation to the case of a person in respect of whom a report has been prepared in accordance with reg.26(3), the fostering panel must either:

  - Request the fostering service provider to prepare a further written report covering all the matters set out in reg.26(2)(c) or
  - Recommend that the person is not suitable to be a foster carer [reg.25(2A) Fostering Services (England) Regulations 2011 as inserted by reg.12 Care Planning and Fostering (Miscellaneous Amendments) (England) Regulations 2015].

Fostering Services (England) Regulations 2011 (as amended)

- The fostering service provider must obtain such information as the fostering panel considers necessary and send that information to the panel, and provide such other assistance as the fostering panel may request, so far as is reasonably practicable [reg.25(3)].

- The fostering panel must also:
  - Advise when appropriate on the procedures under which 'regulation 28' reviews (see below) are carried out by the fostering service provider and periodically monitor their effectiveness
  - Oversee the conduct of assessments carried out by the fostering provider and
  - Give advice and make recommendations on such matters or cases as the fostering service provider may refer to it [reg.25(4)].

NB. In reg.25, 'recommend' means recommend to the fostering service provider [reg.25(5)].

Assessment of Prospective Foster Parents [Reg.26 & Sch.3 Fostering Services (England) Regulations 2011 as substituted by reg.7 Care Planning, Placement and Case Review and Fostering Services (Miscellaneous Amendments) Regulations 2013]

Summary of Key Changes

- The Care Planning, Placement and Case Review and Fostering Services (Miscellaneous Amendments) Regulations 2013 significantly changed the process for assessing prospective foster carers and introduced a shortened process for revising a foster carer's terms of approval subject to her/his agreement.

- The process for assessing a person's suitability to foster consists of two parts. They can be carried out concurrently, but the information required for Stage 1 must be sought as soon as possible, and the decision about whether an applicant has successfully completed Stage 1 must be made within 10 working days of all the information required in that stage being received.

Fostering Services (England) Regulations 2011 (as amended)

- If the fostering service's decision maker decides that the applicant is *not* suitable to foster, s/he must write to the applicant informing her/him of this decision and give full reasons for it. The applicant does not have the right to challenge this decision through the Independent Review Mechanism or by making further representations to the fostering service provider (however, the applicant must be informed that s/he can complain via the fostering service's complaints process if unhappy with the way in which the case has been handled).

- The complaints process should address whether or not the applicant's case has been handled in a reasonable way, rather than the question of the applicant's suitability to foster.

- In the absence of this notification, the fostering service must proceed to Stage 2 of the assessment and a report must be presented to the fostering panel.

- In Stage 2, following a brief or full report being considered by the fostering panel and decision maker, if it is determined that an applicant is not suitable to foster, the applicant must be informed in writing that they may (within 28 calendar days) seek a review of this determination by the IRM or make representations to the provider.

- A fostering service assessing a person's suitability to foster can access the person's previous fostering or adoption records to inform the assessment (subject to relevant consents). When sharing information about individuals applying to foster or adopt, it is important that this is done in a way that protects their personal information.

- If an applicant has been a foster carer in the previous 12 months, and a written reference from her/his previous fostering service is obtained, there is no requirement to also interview personal referees (though there is a power to do so).

- A decision to change a foster carer's terms of approval can now be implemented *immediately* (rather than after 28 days as was previously the case) if the foster carer provides written agreement to the change and there is a written statement concerning the foster family's support needs.

Fostering Services (England) Regulations 2011 (as amended)

Current Regulations

- If a person 'X' applies to become a foster parent and the fostering service provider decides to assess X's ability to become a foster parent, any such assessment must be carried out in accordance with reg.26 [reg.26(1)].

- Subject to reg.26(1B), the fostering service provider must:
  - As soon as reasonably practicable, obtain the information specified in Part 1 of Sch.3 relating to X and other members of X's household and family
  - If X has been a foster parent within the preceding 12 months and was approved as such by another fostering service provider, must request a written reference from that other provider
  - Except where the above situation applies and the other provider provides the requested reference, must interview at least two persons nominated by X to provide personal references for her/him, and prepare written reports of the interviews
  - (Except when the service provider is a local authority and X lives within that authority), consult with and take into account the views of the local authority where X lives and
  - May, if X was approved as a foster parent by another fostering service provider and X consents, request access to the relevant records compiled by that other service provider in relation to X under regs.30 and 31 [reg.26(1A)].

- If, having regard to any information obtained under para.1A, the fostering service provider decides that X is not suitable to become a foster carer or is not suitable by virtue of para. 5–7 (relevant convictions where the exception in para. 8 does *not* apply as described below), the fostering service provider must notify X in writing that s/he is not suitable to be a foster parent, giving reasons for that decision [reg.26(1B)].

- The above notification:
  - May be given notwithstanding that the fostering service provider has not obtained *all* the information set out in para. 1A
  - May not be given more than 10 working days after the fostering service provider has obtained all the information set out in para. 1A.

Fostering Services (England) Regulations 2011 (as amended)

- If the fostering service provider has obtained all the information set out in para. 1A and has not given the notification of para. 1B within the 10 working days of doing so, it must (subject to reg.26(3)):

  - Obtain the information specified in part 2 of Sch.3 relating to X and other household members and any other information it considers relevant
  - Consider whether X is suitable to be a foster parent and whether X's household is suitable for any child
  - Prepare a written report on X which includes the information required by Sch.3 and any other information the provider considers relevant, its assessment of X's suitability to be a foster parent and the provider's proposals about any terms of approval and
  - Notify X that the case is to be referred to the fostering panel, and give X a copy of the above report inviting to send any observations in writing to the fostering service provider within 10 working days, beginning on the date the notification is sent [reg.26(2) as inserted].

- When, having regard to any information obtained under the first of the above bullet points, the fostering service provider decides that X is unlikely to be considered suitable to become a foster parent, it may prepare a written report as per the third bullet point above, even though it may not have obtained all the information about X required by that para [reg.26(3)].

- At the end of the 10 working days referred to in the fourth bullet point above (or when X's observations are received, whichever is the sooner), the provider must send to the fostering panel:

  - The report prepared under reg.26(3)
  - X's observations on that report, if any, and
  - Any other relevant information obtained by the fostering service provider [reg.26(4) as substituted].

- Sch.3 (as amended) specifies the following information which is required with respect to the prospective foster parent:

Fostering Services (England) Regulations 2011 (as amended)

Part 1

- Full name, address and date of birth
- Details of health (supported by a medical report)
- Particulars of other adults in her/his household
- Particulars of the children in the family, whether or not they are members of the household and any other children in the household
- Particulars of her/his accommodation
- The outcome of any request or application made by her/him or any other household member to foster or adopt, or for registration as an early years provider or later years provider under Part 3 Childcare Act 2006, including particulars of any previous approval or refusal of approval relating to her/him or to any other household members
- If X has, in the preceding 12 months, been a foster parent approved by another fostering service provider, the name and address of that provider
- Names and addresses of two persons who will provide personal references for X
- In relation to the prospective foster parent and any other member of her/his household aged 18 or over, an enhanced criminal record certificate issued under s.113B Police Act 1997 that includes suitability information relating to children (as per s.113BA(2) of that Act)
- Details of current and any previous marriage, civil partnership or similar relationship.

Part 2

- Details of personality
- Religious persuasion and capacity to care for a child from any particular religious persuasion
- Racial origin, cultural and linguistic background and capacity to care for a child from any particular such background
- Past and present employment or occupation, standard of living and leisure activities and interests
- Previous experience (if any) of caring for her/his own and other children

- Skills, competence and potential relevant to her/his capacity to care effectively for a child placed with her/him.

■ Subject to reg.26(8), X is *not* suitable to be a foster parent if s/he or any member of the household aged 18 or over:

- Has been convicted of a specified offence committed at the age of 18 or over or
- Has been cautioned by a constable in respect of any such offence [reg.26(5)].

■ In reg.26(5), a 'specified offence' means:

- An offence against a child
- An offence specified in Part 1 Sch.4 (which covers relevant offences in England and Wales, and Scotland and Northern Ireland)
- An offence contrary to s.170 Customs and Excise Management Act 1979 in relation to goods prohibited to be imported under s.42 Customs Consolidation Act 1876 (prohibitions and restrictions relating to pornography) where the prohibited goods included indecent photographs of children aged under 16
- Any other offence including bodily injury to a child other than an offence of common assault or battery.

NB. The expression 'offence against a child' has the meaning given to it by s.26(1) Criminal Justice and Court Service Act 2000 except that it does not include an offence contrary to s.9 Sexual Offences Act 2003 (sexual activity with a child) in a case when the offender was under 20 at the time the offence was committed and the child was aged 13 or over [reg.26(6)].

■ X is not suitable to be a foster parent if X, or any member of X's household aged 18 or over:

- Has been convicted of an offence specified in para. 1 of Part 2 of Sch.4 committed at the age of 18 or over or has been cautioned by a constable, or
- Falls within paras. 2 or 3 of Part 2 of Sch.4, notwithstanding that the statutory offences in Part 2 of Sch.4 have been repealed [reg.26(7)].

Fostering Services (England) Regulations 2011 (as amended)

- The fostering service provider *may* though consider such a person who falls within reg.26(5) 25(7) as suitable to be a foster parent for a particular named child/ren if the service provider is satisfied that the welfare of that child/children requires it and either:

  - The person or a member of her/his household is a relative of the child or
  - The person is already acting as a foster parent for the child [reg.26(8)].
  - In these regulations, a person who is living in X's household in parent and child arrangements is a member of X's household [reg.26(9)].

  NB. In reg.26 and in Sch.4, 'constable' has the meaning given in s.5 Police Act 1993 and for this regulation and regs.27 and 28 and Sch.3 and 5, a person who is living in X's household in 'parent and child arrangements' is a 'member of X's household' [reg.26(9)]. Annex B of Volume 4 provides a fuller explanation of matters relating to parent and children living with foster carers in different circumstances.

Approval of Foster Parent [Reg.27 Fostering Services Regulations (England) 2011]

- A fostering service provider must not approve a person who has been approved as a foster parent by another fostering service provider and whose approval has not been terminated [reg.27(1)].

- A fostering service provider must not approve a person as a foster parent unless:

  - It has completed its assessment of the person's suitability and
  - Its fostering panel has considered the application [reg.27(2)].

- A fostering service provider must, in deciding whether to approve X as a foster parent and as to the terms of any approval, take into account the recommendation of its fostering panel [reg.27(3)].

- No member of its fostering panel shall take part in any decision made by a fostering service provider under reg.27(3) [reg.27(4)].

Fostering Services (England) Regulations 2011 (as amended)

- If a fostering service provider decides to approve a person as a foster parent, it must:
  - Give X notice in writing, specifying any terms on which the approval is given
  - Enter into a written agreement with X covering the matters specified in Sch. 5 (the 'foster care agreement') summarised immediately below [reg.27(5)].

Matters & Obligations in Foster Care Agreements [Sch.5 in support of Reg.27(5) Fostering Services Regulations (England) 2011]

Matters to be recorded

- Terms of the foster parent's approval
- Amount of support and training to be given to the foster parent
- Procedure for the review of approval of a foster parent
- Procedure in connection with the placement of children and the matters to be included in any placement plan
- Arrangements for meeting any legal liabilities of the foster parent arising by reason of a placement
- Procedure available to foster parents for making representations.

Obligations on the foster parent

- To care for any child placed with her/him as if the child was a child of the foster parent's family and to promote that child's welfare, having regard to the long and short-term plans for the child.

- To give written notice to the fostering service provider without delay, with full particulars of:
  - Any intended change of the foster parent's address
  - Any change in the composition of the household, any other change in her/his personal circumstances and any other event affecting either their capacity to care for any child placed or the suitability of the household, and any request or application to adopt children, or for registration as an early years or later years provider under Part 3 Childcare Act 2006.

Fostering Services (England) Regulations 2011 (as amended)

- To:

  - Agree not to administer corporal punishment to any child placed with the foster parent
  - Ensure that any information relating to a child placed with the foster parent, to the child's family or to any other person, which has been given to her/him in confidence in connection with a placement is kept confidential and is not disclosed to any person without the consent of the fostering service provider
  - Comply with the terms of any placement plan
  - Comply with the policies and procedures of the fostering service provider issued under regs.12 and 13
  - Co-operate as reasonably required with the Chief Inspector, and in particular to allow a person authorised by the Chief Inspector to interview the foster parent and visit the foster parent's home at any reasonable time
  - Keep the fostering service provider informed about the child's progress and to notify it as soon as is reasonably practicable of any significant events affecting the child.

Qualifying Determination

- If a fostering service provider considers that a person is *not* suitable to act as a foster parent, it must, subject to reg.27(7):

  - Give X written notice that it proposes not to approve her/him as suitable to act as a foster parent ('a qualifying determination'), together with its reasons and a copy of the fostering panel's recommendation, and
  - Advise the person that within 28 days of the qualifying determination, X may submit any written representations s/he wishes to make to the fostering service provider, or apply to the Secretary of State for a review by an independent review panel of the determination [reg.27(6)].

- The option of applying to the Secretary of State does not apply in a case where the fostering service provider considers in accordance with

Fostering Services (England) Regulations 2011 (as amended)

reg.26(8) that the person is not suitable to act as a foster parent [reg.27(7)].

- The fostering service provider may proceed to make its decision if, within the 28 day period:
  - It does not receive any representations, and
  - The person does not apply to the Secretary of State for a review by an independent review panel of the qualifying determination [reg.27(8)].

- If, within the 28 day period, the fostering service provider receives any written representations, it must:
  - Refer the case to the fostering panel for further consideration and
  - Make its decision, taking into account any fresh recommendation made by the fostering panel [reg.27(9)].

- If, within the 28 day period, the person applies to the Secretary of State for a review by an independent review panel of the qualifying determination, the fostering service provider must make its decision, taking into account the recommendation of the fostering panel and the recommendation of the independent review panel [reg.27(10)].

- As soon as practicable after making one of the relevant decisions referred to above, the fostering service provider must notify the prospective foster parent in writing and:
  - If the decision is to approve X as a foster parent, comply with reg.27(5) (specifying approval and its terms etc) in relation to the person or
  - If the decision is not to approve the person, provide written reasons for its decision [reg.27(11)].

- In a case when an independent review panel has made a recommendation, the fostering service provider must send to the Secretary of State a copy of the notification referred to in reg.27(11) [reg.27(12)].

Fostering Services (England) Regulations 2011 (as amended)

Reviews & Terminations of Approval [Reg.28 Fostering Services (England) Regulations 2011 as amended]

- The fostering service provider must review the approval of each foster parent in accordance with this regulation [reg.28(1)].

- A review must take place not more than one year after approval, and thereafter whenever the fostering service provider considers it necessary, but at intervals of not more than one year [reg.28(2)].

- When undertaking a review, the fostering service provider must:
  - Make such enquiries and obtain such information as it considers necessary in order to review whether the foster parent continues to be suitable to be a foster parent and the foster parent's household continues to be suitable; and
  - Seek and take into account the views of the foster parent and (subject to the child's age and understanding) any child placed with the foster parent and any placing authority which has within the preceding year placed a child with the foster parent [reg.28(3)].

- At the conclusion of the review, the fostering service provider must prepare a written report, setting out whether the:
  - Foster parent continues to be suitable to act as a foster parent and the foster parent's household continues to be suitable and
  - Terms of the foster parent's approval continue to be appropriate [reg.28(4)].

- The fostering service provider must on the occasion of the first review under this regulation, and may on any subsequent review, refer its report to the fostering panel for consideration [reg.28(5)].

- If the fostering service provider decides, taking into account any recommendation made by the panel, that the foster parent and the foster parent's household continue to be suitable and that the terms of the foster parent's approval continue to be appropriate, it must give written notice to the foster parent of its decision [reg.28(6)].

- If, taking into account any recommendation made by the fostering panel, the service provider is no longer satisfied the foster parent or the foster parent's household continue to be suitable, or that the terms of the approval are appropriate, it must (subject to reg.28(8):

- Give written notice to the foster parent that it proposes to terminate, or (as the case may be) revise the terms of approval ('a qualifying determination'), together with its reasons and a copy of any recommendation made by the fostering panel, and
- Advise the foster parent that within 28 days of the date of the notice the foster parent may submit any written representations s/he wishes to make to the fostering service provider, or apply to the Secretary of State for a review by an independent review panel of the qualifying determination [reg.28(7)].

■ In any case when the fostering service provider proposes only to revise the terms of the foster parent's approval, it must provide a statement setting out whether the provider considers that the foster parent or members of her/his household (including any placed children) may have additional support needs as a result of the proposed revision; and if so how they will be met and request the foster parent's agreement in writing to the proposed revision of terms [reg.28(7)(aa) as inserted by reg.8 Care Planning, Placement and Case Review and Fostering Services (Miscellaneous Amendments) Regulations 2013].

NB. When the fostering service provider receives the carer's written agreement to the variation it may, taking account of any additional support needs, proceed with its decision as above without waiting for 28 days [reg.28(9A)].

■ The option of applying to the Secretary of State does not apply in a case when, in accordance with reg.26(8), the fostering service provider is no longer satisfied that the foster parent and her/his household continue to be suitable, or that the terms of the approval are appropriate [reg.28(8)].

■ The fostering service provider may proceed to make its decision if, within the 28 day period, the:

- Fostering service provider does not receive any representations, and

- Foster parent does not apply to the Secretary of State for a review by an independent review panel of the qualifying determination [reg.28(9)].

■ If, within the 28 day period, the fostering service provider receives any written representations, it must:

- Refer the case to the fostering panel for its consideration and
- Make its decision, taking into account any recommendation made by the fostering panel [reg.28(10)].

■ If the foster parent applies within the 28 day period to the Secretary of State for a review by an independent review panel of the qualifying determination, the fostering service provider must make its decision taking into account any recommendation made by its fostering panel and the recommendation of the independent review panel [reg.28(11)].

■ As soon as practicable after making any of the decisions referred to above, the fostering service provider must give written notice to the foster parent stating (as the case may be):

- That the foster parent and the foster parent's household continue to be suitable, and that the terms of the approval continue to be appropriate
- That the foster parent's approval is terminated from a specified date, and the reasons for the termination or
- Revised terms of the approval and the reasons for the revision [reg.28(12)].

■ A foster parent may give notice in writing to the fostering service provider at any time that s/he no longer wishes to act as a foster parent, whereupon the foster parent's approval is terminated with effect from 28 days from the date on which the notice is received by the fostering service provider [reg.28(13)].

■ A copy of any notice given under reg.28 must be sent to the placing authority for any child placed with the foster parent (unless the placing authority is also the fostering service provider), and the area authority [reg.28(14)].

Fostering Services (England) Regulations 2011 (as amended)

- In a case when an independent review panel has made a recommendation, the fostering service provider must send to the Secretary of State a copy of the notification referred to in reg.28(12) [reg.28(15)].

Information to be sent to the Independent Panel [Reg.29 Fostering Services (England) Regulations 2011]

- Reg.29 applies when the fostering service provider receives notification from the Secretary of State that a person has applied for a review by an independent review panel of a determination [reg.29(1)].

- The fostering service provider must, within 10 working days of receipt of that notification, send to the Secretary of State the following documents:

  - A copy of any report prepared, and of any other documents referred to the fostering panel, for the purposes of regs.26, 27 or 28, as the case may be
  - Any relevant information in relation to the person obtained by the fostering service provider after the date on which the report was prepared or the documents referred to the fostering panel and
  - A copy of the notice and any other documents sent in accordance with reg.27(6)(a) or reg.28(7)(a) (qualifying determinations) [reg.29(2);(3)].

Case Records Relating to Foster Parents & Others [Reg.30 Fostering Services (England) Regulations 2011]

- A fostering service provider must maintain a case record for each foster parent approved by it, which must include copies of the documents specified in reg.30(2) and the information specified in reg.30(3):

  - The report prepared under reg.26(3)(b) and any other reports submitted to the fostering panel
  - Any recommendations made by the fostering panel
  - Notice of approval given under reg.27(5)(a)
  - Foster care agreement
  - Any report of a review of approval prepared under reg.28(4)
  - Any notice given under reg.28(12) [reg.30(1);(2).

Fostering Services (England) Regulations 2011 (as amended)

- The information referred to in reg.30(1) is, as the case may be:
    - A record of each placement with the foster parent, including name, age and sex of each child placed, dates on which each placement began and terminated and the circumstances of the termination
    - The information obtained by the fostering service provider in relation to the assessment and approval of the foster parent and in relation to any review or termination of the approval [reg.30(3)].

- A local authority is obliged to maintain a case record for each person with whom a child is placed under reg.24 of the Care Planning, Placement and Review (England) Regulations 2010 (temporary approval of relative, friend or other person connected with the child), or reg.25A of those regulations (temporary approval of prospective adopter as a foster parent) which must include in relation to that person:
    - A record in relation to the placement, including the name, age and sex of each child placed, dates on which the placement began and terminated, and the circumstances of the termination, and
    - The information obtained in relation to the enquiries carried out under reg.24(2) or reg.25A (as appropriate) of the Care Planning Regulations [reg.30(4)].

- The fostering service provider must compile a record for each person whom it does not approve as a foster parent, or who withdraws her/his application prior to approval, which must include in relation to her/him:
    - The information obtained in connection with the assessment
    - Any report submitted to and any recommendation made by the fostering panel and
    - Any notification given under reg.27 [reg.30(5)].

Register of Foster Parents [Reg.31 Fostering Services (England) Regulations 2011 as amended]

- The fostering service provider must maintain a register (a register of foster parents) and enter in it the following particulars:
    - Name, address, date of birth and sex of each foster parent (and in the case of a local authority fostering service, of each person with whom

Fostering Services (England) Regulations 2011 (as amended)

it has placed a child under reg.24 or reg.25A of the Care Planning Regulations)
- Date of her/his approval and of each review of her/his approval (as the case may be) and
- Current terms of her/his approval (if any) [reg.31].

Retention & Confidentiality of Records [Reg.32 Fostering Services (England) Regulations 2011 as amended]

- Records compiled in relation to a foster parent under reg.30(1), and any entry relating to her/him in the register maintained under reg.31, must be retained for at least 10 years from the date on which approval is terminated [reg.32(1)].

- Records compiled by a local authority under reg.30(4) in relation to a person with whom a child is placed under reg.24 or reg.25A of the Care Planning Regulations, and any entry relating to such a person in the register maintained under reg.31, must be retained for at least 10 years from the date on which the placement is terminated [reg.32(2)].

- Records compiled under reg.30(5) must be retained for at least three years from refusal or withdrawal of the application to become a foster parent [reg.32(3)].

- These requirements may be complied with by retaining the original written records or copies, or by keeping all or part of the information contained in them in another accessible form, e.g. computer record [reg.32(4)].

- Subject to reg.32(6), any records or register maintained in accordance with regs.30 or 31 must be kept securely and may not be disclosed to any person except in accordance with any:

  - Provision of, or made under, or by virtue of, a statute under which access to such records is authorised or any
  - Court order authorising access to such records [reg.32(5)].

- A fostering service provider must provide access to its records complied under regs.30 or 31 in relation to a foster parent to another fostering service provider within 15 working days of a request under reg.26(1A) or

Fostering Services (England) Regulations 2011 (as amended)

an adoption agency within 15 working days of a request under reg.30F(4) of the Adoption Agencies Regulations 2005 [reg.32(6) as substituted].

Fostering Agencies: Miscellaneous [Regs.33–41 Fostering Services (England) Regulations 2011]

Fostering Agency Ceasing to Carry Out Fostering Functions: Notifications & Records [Reg.33 Fostering Services (England) Regulations 2011]

- If a fostering agency is to cease carrying out the functions of a fostering agency ('the old agency'), the registered provider must, without delay, notify the following of that fact:
  - The local authority fostering service in whose area the old agency is situated
  - The Chief Inspector
  - Every foster parent currently approved by the old agency under reg.27 and every other foster parent for whom the old agency has responsibility by virtue of reg.33(2)
  - The responsible authority, and if different, the placing authority for every child currently placed with a foster parent falling within the above bullet.

- In the case of the latter two notifications, the fostering agency must also confirm the identity of the new fostering service [reg.33(1)].

- The registered provider of the old agency may agree with a local authority fostering service, or another fostering agency that that fostering service will become the fostering service ('the new fostering service') in relation to some or all of its foster parents and, in the absence of such agreement, the local authority fostering service in whose area each foster parent lives will become the new fostering service in relation to them [reg.33(2)].

Fostering Services (England) Regulations 2011 (as amended)

- The registered provider of the closing agency must arrange for the records of the closing agency maintained by virtue of reg.30 in relation to its foster parents to be passed to the relevant new fostering agency before the date on which the closing agency closes [reg.33(4)].

- A responsible authority notified under reg.33(1) must inform the IRO for each child placed by it of the fact that the closing agency is closing and the identity of the new fostering service for that child's foster parent [reg.33(5)].

Fostering Agency Ceasing to Carry Out Fostering Functions: New Fostering Service Providers [Reg.34 Fostering Services (England) Regulations 2011]

- Unless it is not reasonably practicable to do so, the fostering service provider in relation to a new fostering service ('the new fostering service provider') must, within 16 weeks of the date on which the old agency closes, carry out an assessment of any foster parent for whom it has assumed responsibility by virtue of reg.33(2) or (3) (a 'transferred foster parent') and decide whether to approve her/him as a foster parent in accordance with the provisions of regs.26 and 27, with the modification that reg.27(1) (preventing contemporaneous approval by two agencies/services) does not apply [reg.34(1)].

- Subject to reg.34(3), if the new fostering service provider carries out the assessment in reg.34(1) and does not approve the transferred foster parent, or fails to carry out the assessment within 16 weeks, the transferred foster parent's approval is terminated [reg.34(2)].

- If it is not reasonably practicable for the new fostering service provider to complete its assessment and make its decision with 16 weeks, the transferred foster parent's approval may be extended for such period as is necessary for the fostering service provider to make its decision [reg.34(3)].

Review of Quality of Care: [Reg.35 & Sch. 6 Fostering Services (England) Regulations 2011]

- The registered person must establish and maintain a system for:

Fostering Services (England) Regulations 2011 (as amended)

- Monitoring the matters set out in Sch. 6 (summarised immediately below) at appropriate intervals, and
- Improving the quality of foster care provided by the fostering agency [reg.35(1)].

■ The registered person must provide the Chief Inspector with a written report in respect of any review conducted by her/him for the purposes of reg.35(1) and, on request, to any local authority [reg.35(2)].

■ The system referred to in reg.35(1) must provide for consultation with foster parents, children placed with foster parents, and their placing authority (unless, in the case of a fostering agency which is a voluntary organisation, it is also the responsible authority).

Matters to be monitored by the Registered Person [Sch.6 in Support of Reg.35(1) Fostering Services (England) Regulations 2011]

■ Compliance in relation to each child placed with foster parents, with the child's care plan.

■ All accidents, injuries and illnesses of children placed with foster parents.

■ Complaints in relation to children placed with foster parents and their outcomes.

■ Any allegations or suspicions of abuse in respect of children placed with foster parents and the outcome of any investigation.

■ Recruitment records and conduct of required checks of new workers.

■ Notifications of events listed in Schedule 7.

■ Any unauthorised absence from the foster home of a child accommodated there.

■ Use of any measures of control, restraint or discipline in respect of children accommodated in a foster home.

■ Medication, medical treatment and first aid administered to any child placed with foster parents.

Fostering Services (England) Regulations 2011 (as amended)

- Where applicable, the standard of any education provided by the fostering service.
- Records of assessments.
- Records of fostering panel meetings.
- Records of appraisals of employees.
- Minutes of staff meetings.

Notifiable Events: [Reg.36 Fostering Services (England) Regulations 2011]

- If, in relation to a fostering agency, any of the events listed in column 1 of the table in Sch.7 (summarised) takes place, the registered person must without delay notify the persons or bodies indicated in respect of the event in column 2 of the table [reg.36(1)]. Any notification made in accordance with this regulation which is given orally must be confirmed in writing [reg.36(2)].

Fostering Services (England) Regulations 2011 (as amended)

Event	To be notified to					
	Chief Inspector	Responsible authority	Secretary of State	Area authority	Police	CCG
Child's death	✓	✓	✓	✓		✓
Information is provided to ISA under either s.35,36,39,41 or 45 Safeguarding Vulnerable Groups Act 2006 in respect of an individual working for a fostering service	✓	✓				
Serious illness/accident of placed child	✓	✓				✓
Outbreak at foster home of any infectious disease which in opinion of an attending GP is sufficiently serious to be so notified	✓	✓				
Allegation of serious crime by child		✓			✓	
Involvement or suspected involvement of child in sexual exploitation	✓	✓		✓	✓	
Serious incident with police attending foster home	✓	✓				
Missing from placement		✓		✓	✓	
Any serious complaint re: foster parent	✓	✓				
Instigation & outcome any protection enquiry	✓	✓		✓		

Fostering Services (England) Regulations 2011 (as amended)

Financial Position [Reg.37 Fostering Services (England) Regulations 2011]

- The registered provider must carry on the fostering agency in such manner as is likely to ensure that it will be financially viable for the purpose of achieving the aims and objectives set out in its statement of purpose [reg.37(1)].
- The registered provider must:
  - Ensure that adequate accounts are maintained and kept up to date in respect of the fostering agency, and
  - Supply a copy of the accounts, if requested to do so, to the Chief Inspector [reg.37(2)].
- The registered provider must, if the Chief Inspector so requests, provide her/him with such information as s/he may require for the purpose of considering the financial viability of the fostering agency, including:
  - The annual accounts of the fostering agency certified by an accountant
  - A reference from a bank expressing an opinion as to the registered provider's financial standing
  - Information as to the financing and financial resources of the fostering agency
  - (If the registered provider is a company) information as to any of its associated companies, and
  - A certificate of insurance for the registered provider in respect of liability which may be incurred by her/him in relation to the fostering agency in respect of death, injury, public liability, damage or other loss [reg.37(3)].
- In reg.37, a company is associated with another if one of them has control of the other, or both are under the control of the same person [reg.37(4)].

Notice of Absence [Reg.38 Fostering Services (England) Regulations 2011]

- If a registered manager proposes to be absent from the fostering agency for a continuous period of 28 days or more, the registered person must give notice in writing to the Chief Inspector of the proposed absence [reg.38(1)].

- Except in the case of an emergency, the notice referred to in reg.38(1) must be given no later than one month before the proposed absence is to start, or within such shorter period as may be agreed with the Chief Inspector, and the notice must specify:
  - Length or expected length of the proposed absence
  - Reason for the proposed absence
  - Arrangements which have been made for the running of the fostering agency during that absence
  - Name, address and qualifications of the person who will be responsible for the fostering agency during the absence, and
  - Arrangements that have been made or are proposed to be made for appointing another person to manage the fostering agency during the absence, including the proposed date by which the appointment is to start [reg.38(2)].

- If the absence arises as a result of an emergency, the registered person must give notice of the absence within one week of its occurrence, specifying all the matters mentioned in reg.38(2) [reg.38(3)].

- If the registered manager has been absent from the fostering agency for a continuous period of 28 days or more, and the Chief Inspector has not been given notice of the absence, the registered person must without delay give notice in writing to the Chief Inspector specifying the matters mentioned in reg.38(2) [reg.38(4)].

- The registered person must notify the Chief Inspector of the return to duty of the registered manager not later than seven days after the date of her/his return [reg.38(5)].

Notice of Changes [Reg.39 Fostering Services (England) Regulations 2011]

- The registered person must give notice in writing to the Chief Inspector as soon as it is practicable to do so if any of the following events takes place or is proposed to take place:

- A person other than the registered person carries on or manages the fostering agency
- A person ceases to carry on or manage the fostering agency
- Where the registered provider is an individual, s/he changes her/his name
- If the registered provider is a partnership, there is any change in the membership of the partnership,
- If the registered provider is an organisation, the name or address of the organisation is changed, there is any change of director, manager, secretary or other similar officer of the organisation or there is to be any change in the identity of the responsible individual
- If the registered provider is an individual, a trustee in bankruptcy is appointed or s/he makes any composition or arrangement with her/his creditors, or
- If the registered provider is a company or a partnership, a receiver, manager, liquidator or provisional liquidator is appointed in respect of the registered provider [reg.39(1)].

■ The registered provider must notify the Chief Inspector in writing and without delay of the death of the registered manager [reg.39(2)].

Appointment of Liquidators etc [Reg.40 Fostering Services (England) Regulations 2011]

■ Any person to whom reg.40(2) applies must:

- As soon as is reasonably practicable, notify the Chief Inspector of her/his appointment, indicating the reasons for it
- Appoint a manager to take full-time day to day charge of the fostering agency in any case where there is no registered manager, and
- Not more than 28 days after appointment, notify the Chief Inspector of her/his intentions regarding the future operation of the fostering agency [reg.40(1)].

■ Reg.40(2) applies to any person appointed as:

- The receiver or manager of the property of a company or partnership which is a registered provider of a fostering agency

- A liquidator or provisional liquidator of a company which is the registered provider of a fostering agency, or
- The trustee in bankruptcy of a registered provider of a fostering agency [reg.40(2)].

Compliance with Regulations [Reg.41 Fostering Services (England) Regulations 2011]

■ If there is more than one registered person in respect of a fostering agency, anything which is required under these Regulations to be done by the registered person, need only be done by one of the registered persons.

Application of these Regulations with Modifications to Short Breaks [Reg.42 Fostering Services (England) Regulations 2011]

■ In the circumstances set out in reg.42(2), these regulations apply in relation to a child with the modifications set out in reg.42(3) [reg.42(1)].

■ The circumstances are that the child:

- Is *not* in the care of a local authority, i.e. is 'accommodated', and
- Is placed in a series of short-term placements with the same foster parent ('short breaks'), where no single placement is intended to last for more than 17 days, at the end of each such placement returns to the care of the child's parent or a person who is not her/his parent but who has parental responsibility for the child and that the short breaks do not exceed 75 days in total in any period of 12 months [reg.42(2)].

■ The modifications are that:

- Regs.14,15(2)(a) and (d), and 16 do not apply in relation to the child.

NATIONAL MINIMUM STANDARDS (NMS)

National Minimum Standards (NMS)

Values/Principles

- The child's welfare, safety and needs are at the centre of their care.
- Children should have an enjoyable childhood and benefit from excellent parenting and education, enjoying a wide range of opportunities to develop their talents and skills, leading to a successful adult life.
- Children are entitled to grow up in a loving environment that can meet their developmental needs.
- Every child should have her/his wishes and feelings listened to and taken into account.
- Each child should be valued as an individual and given personalised support in line with their individual needs and background in order to develop their identity, self-confidence and self-worth.
- The particular needs of disabled children and children with complex needs will be fully recognised and taken into account.
- The significance of contact for looked after children, and of maintaining relationships with birth parents and the wider family, including siblings, half-siblings and grandparents, is recognised, as is the foster carer's role in this.
- Children in foster care deserve to be treated as a good parent would treat their own children and to have the opportunity for as full an experience of family life and childhood as possible without unnecessary restrictions.
- The central importance of the child's relationship with her/his foster carer should be acknowledged and foster carers should be recognised as a core member of the team around the child.
- Foster carers have a right to full information about the child.
- It is essential that foster carers receive relevant support services and development opportunities in order to provide the best care for children.

National Minimum Standards (NMS)

- A genuine partnership between all those involved in fostering children is essential for the National Minimum Standards (NMS) to deliver the best outcomes for children; this includes the government, local government, other statutory agencies, fostering service providers and foster carers.

Legal Status of the National Minimum Standards

- The NMS for fostering services are issued by the Secretary of State under s.23 Care Standards Act 2000. The Secretary of State will keep the standards under review and may publish amended standards as appropriate.
- Minimum standards do not mean standardisation of provision. The standards are designed to be applicable to the wide variety of different types of fostering service. They aim to enable, rather than prevent, individual providers to develop their own particular ethos and approach based on evidence that this is the most appropriate way to meet the child's needs. Many providers will aspire to exceed these standards and develop their service in order to achieve excellence.
- The standards are issued for use by the Chief Inspector (Ofsted), who will take them into account in the inspection of fostering services. They will also be important in other ways. The standards may be used by providers and staff in self-assessment of their services; they provide a basis for the induction and training of staff and carers; they can be used by parents, children and young people as a guide to what they should expect a fostering service to provide and to do as a minimum; and they can provide guidance on what is required when setting up a fostering service.

National Minimum Standards (NMS)

Structure & Approach to Inspection

- The NMS for fostering focus on delivering achievable outcomes for children.
- Each standard is preceded by a statement of the outcome to be achieved by the fostering service provider.
- The standards are intended to be qualitative, in that they provide a tool for judging the quality of life experienced by services users, but they are also designed to be measurable.
- Services will normally show that they are meeting the headline statement of outcome by following the standards below. However, these do not have to be followed to the letter if the service can demonstrate, and the Chief Inspector is satisfied, that the outcomes are being met in a different way.
- Such variation/flexibility may be appropriate in services with specific purposes, for example, the provision of short breaks for disabled children. The exception is a requirement set out in regulations, in which case the regulation must be met. The underpinning regulatory requirement is provided at the beginning of each standard.
- Across all its work, Ofsted has three statutory responsibilities under s.117 Education & Inspections Act 2006:
  - To ensure that inspection supports improvements in the services the Chief Inspector inspects and regulates
  - That it is centred on the needs of users
  - It promotes the effective use of resources.
- There are four elements to Ofsted's functions as a regulator: registration; inspection; compliance; and enforcement. The purpose of Ofsted's inspection of social care is to assess the quality of care being provided for children and, where appropriate, their families.

National Minimum Standards (NMS)

- Inspection focuses on the outcomes which they are being supported to achieve. It tests compliance with the relevant regulations, and takes into account the NMS.
- Following inspection, inspectors will make a number of judgements, including a judgement on the overall effectiveness of the service inspected. They will make recommendations for improvement, including any action required to ensure that provisions fully meet the NMS.
- For those provisions which are required to be registered with the Chief Inspector, they will set requirements to be fulfilled in order to remedy any identified failure to meet the relevant regulations. Any identified failure in meeting the requirements of regulations may lead to consideration of enforcement action. Conditions of registration may be imposed.

The Wider Context

- These NMS are underpinned by the Fostering Services Regulations 2011 (as amended). Statutory guidance for fostering sets out the wider context for local authorities, as providers and commissioners of fostering services. This is not an exhaustive list, and other legislation and guidance may also be relevant, for example, legislation covering such matters as health and safety, fire or planning requirements.
- It is intended that the standards will be used, both by fostering service providers and by the Chief Inspector, to focus on securing positive welfare, health and education outcomes for children, and reducing risks to their welfare and safety.
- All providers and staff of fostering services should aim to provide the best care possible for the children for whom they are responsible, and observing the standards is an essential part, but only a part, of the overall responsibility to safeguard and promote the welfare of each individual child.

Application to Short Breaks

- Both the Fostering Services Regulations 2011 and the NMS are modified in relation to short breaks. This is in recognition that where the child receives short breaks, the parents have primary responsibility for planning for their child.

- Short break care is defined in reg.42 Fostering Services Regulations 2011 and the modifications are that regs.14, 15(2)(a) and (d), and 16 do not apply in relation to the child, and the procedure referred to in regulation 16(2)(a) does not apply to the child.

- The following NMS do not apply in relation to short break care: standard 2.5, 2.7 and all of standards 9 and 12.

- In addition, there is no requirement for a separate placement plan for children looked after in a series of short breaks (Care Planning, Placement and Case Review (England) Regulations (2010), reg.48(3)). For such children, the short break care plan includes key elements of the placement plan. Where the NMS state 'placement plan', this will be the short break care plan in relation to children on short breaks.

NB. The wording of the following standards has on occasions been amended to make their meaning clearer.

CHILD-FOCUSED STANDARDS

Child-Focused Standards

Standard 1 – Child's Wishes & Feelings & Views of Those Significant to Her/Him

Underpinning Legislation

Regulation 11 – Independent fostering agencies – Duty to secure welfare
Regulation 18 – Independent fostering agencies – Representations & complaints
s.22 CA 1989 – General duties of local authority in relation to children looked after by it
ss.61 & 62 – Duties of voluntary organisations and local authorities in relation to children accommodated by or on behalf of the voluntary organisation

Outcome

Children know that their views, wishes and feelings are taken into account in all aspects of their care, are helped to understand why it may not be possible to act upon their wishes in all cases; and know how to obtain support and make a complaint. The views of others with an important relationship to the child are gathered and taken into account.

Standard

1.1 Children's view, wishes and feelings are acted upon, unless this is contrary to their interests or adversely affects other members of the foster care household.

1.2 Children understand how their views have been taken into account and, where significant wishes or concerns are not acted upon, they are helped to understand why.

1.3 Children communicate their views on all aspects of their care and support.

1.4 The views of the child, the child's family, social worker and IRO are sought regularly on the child's care (unless in individual cases this is not appropriate).

Child-Focused Standards

1.5 Children have access to independent advice and support from adults who they can contact directly and in private about problems or concerns, which is appropriate to their age and understanding. Children know their rights to advocacy and how to access an advocate, and how to contact the Children's Commissioner.

1.6 Children can take up issues in the most appropriate way with support, without fear that this will result in any adverse consequences. Children receive prompt feedback on any concerns or complaints raised and are kept informed of progress.

1.7 The wishes, feelings and views of children and those significant to them are taken into account in monitoring foster carers and developing the fostering service.

Standard 2 – Promoting a Positive Identity, Potential & Valuing Diversity through Individualised Care

Underpinning Legislation

Regulation 11 – Independent fostering agencies – Duty to secure welfare
s.22 CA 1989 – General duties of local authority in relation to children looked after by it
ss.61 & 62 – Duties of voluntary organisations and local authorities in relation to children accommodated by or on behalf of the voluntary organisation

Outcome

Children have a positive self view, emotional resilience and knowledge and understanding of their background.

Child-Focused Standards

Standard

2.1 Children are provided with personalised care that meets their needs and promotes all aspects of their individual identity.

2.2 Foster carers are supported to promote children's social and emotional development, and to enable children to develop emotional resilience and positive self-esteem.

2.3 Foster carers meet children's individual needs as set out in the child's placement plan as part of the wider family context.

2.4 Children exercise choice in the food that they eat, and are able to prepare their own meals and snacks, within the context of the foster family's decision making and the limits that a responsible parent would set.

2.5 Children exercise choice and independence in the clothes and personal requisites that they buy and have these needs met, within the context of the foster family's decision making and the reasonable limits that a responsible parent would set. **This sub-standard is not applicable to short break placements.**

2.6 Children develop skills and emotional resilience that will prepare them for independent living.

2.7 Children receive a personal allowance appropriate to their age and understanding that is consistent with their placement plan. **This sub-standard is not applicable to short break placements.**

Standard 3 – Promoting Positive Behaviour & Relationships

Underpinning Legislation

Regulation 11 – Independent fostering agencies – Duty to secure welfare
Regulation 13 – Behaviour management & absence from foster carer's home

Child-Focused Standards

Regulation 17 – Support, training & information for foster carer's activities
s.22 CA 1989 – General duties of local authority in relation to children looked after by it
s.61 and 62 – Duties of voluntary organisations and local authorities in relation to children accommodated by or on behalf of the voluntary organisation

Outcome

Children enjoy sound relationships with their foster family, interact positively with others and behave appropriately.

Standard

3.1 Foster carers have high expectations of all of the foster children in their household.

3.2 Foster carers provide an environment and culture that promotes, models and supports positive behaviour.

3.3 Children are able to develop and practise skills to build and maintain positive relationships, be assertive and to resolve conflicts positively.

3.4 Children are encouraged to take responsibility for their behaviour in a way that is appropriate to their age and abilities.

3.5 Foster carers respect the child's privacy and confidentiality, in a manner consistent with good parenting.

3.6 Foster carers have positive strategies for effectively supporting children where they encounter discrimination or bullying, wherever this occurs.

3.7 Foster carers receive support on how to manage their responses and feelings arising from caring for children, particularly where children display very challenging behaviour and understand how children's previous experiences can manifest in challenging behaviour.

3.8 All foster carers receive training in positive care and control of children, including training in de-escalating problems and disputes. The fostering service has a clear written policy on managing behaviour, which includes supporting positive behaviour, de-escalation of conflicts, and discipline.

Child-Focused Standards

The fostering service's policy is made clear to the responsible/placing authority, child and parent/s or carers before the placement begins or, in an emergency placement, at the time of the placement.

3.9 Each foster carer is aware of all the necessary information available to the fostering service about a child's circumstances, including any significant recent events, to help the foster carer understand, predict and support the child's needs and behaviours within their household. The fostering service follows up with the responsible authority if all such necessary information has not been provided by the authority.

3.10 The fostering service's approach to care minimises the need for police involvement to deal with challenging behaviour and avoids criminalising children unnecessarily.

Standard 4 – Protecting from Abuse & Neglect

Underpinning Legislation

Regulation 11 – Independent fostering agencies – Duty to secure welfare
Regulation 12 – Arrangements for the protection of children

Outcome

Children feel safe and are safe; children understand how to protect themselves and are protected from significant harm including neglect, abuse and accident.

Standard

4.1 Children's safety and welfare is promoted in all fostering placements. Children are protected from abuse and other forms of significant harm, e.g. sexual or labour exploitation.

4.2 Foster carers actively safeguard and promote the welfare of foster children.

Child-Focused Standards

4.3 Foster carers make positive relationships with children, generate a culture of openness and trust and are aware of and alert to any signs or symptoms that might indicate a child is at risk of harm.

4.4 Foster carers encourage children to take appropriate risks as a normal part of growing up. Children are helped to understand how to keep themselves safe, including when outside of the household or when using the internet or social media.

4.5 The service implements a proportionate approach to any risk assessment.

4.6 Foster carers are trained in appropriate safer-care practice, including skills to care for children who have been abused. For foster carers who offer placements to disabled children, this includes training specifically on issues affecting disabled children.

4.7 The fostering service works effectively in partnership with other agencies concerned with child protection, e.g. the responsible authority, schools, hospitals, general practitioners, etc, and does not work in isolation from them.

Standard 5 – Children Missing from Care

Underpinning Legislation

Regulation 13 – Behaviour management and absence from foster parent's home

Outcome

Children rarely go missing and if they do, return quickly. Children who do go missing are protected as far as possible and responded to positively on their return.

Child-Focused Standards

Standard

5.1 The care and support provided to children minimises the risk that they will go missing and reduces the risk of harm should the child go missing.

5.2 Foster carers know and implement what the fostering service and the responsible authority's policy is in relation to children going missing.

5.3 Foster carers are aware of and do not exceed the measures they can take to prevent a child leaving without permission under current legislation and government guidance.

5.4 Children who are absent from the foster home without consent but whose whereabouts are known or thought to be known by carers or staff are protected in line with the fostering service's written procedure.

5.5 The fostering service and foster carers take appropriate action to find children who are missing, including working alongside the police where appropriate.

5.6 If a child is absent from the fostering home and her/his whereabouts are not known, i.e. the child is missing, the fostering service's procedures are compatible with the local 'Runaway and Missing from Home and Care' (RMFHC) protocols and procedures applicable to the area where each foster home is located.

5.7 Where children placed out of authority go missing, the registered manager of the fostering service follows the local RMFHC protocol. They also comply with and make foster carers aware of any other processes required by the placing authority, specified in the individual child's care plan and in the RMFHC protocol covering the authority responsible for the child's care.

5.8 Children are helped to understand the dangers and risks of leaving the foster home without permission and are made aware of where they can access help if they consider running away.

5.9 Where a child goes missing and there is concern for their welfare, or at the request of a child who has been missing, the fostering service arranges a meeting in private between the child and the responsible authority to consider the reasons for their going missing. The fostering

Child-Focused Standards

service considers with the responsible authority and foster carer what action should be taken to prevent the child going missing in future. Any concerns arising about the foster carer or the placement are addressed, as far as is possible, in conjunction with the responsible authority.

5.10 Written records kept by the fostering service where a child goes missing detail action taken by foster carers, the circumstances of the child's return, any reasons given by the child for running away from the foster home and any action taken in the light of those reasons. This information is shared with the responsible authority and, where appropriate, the child's parents.

Standard 6 – Promoting Good Health & Wellbeing

Underpinning Legislation

Regulation 15 – Health of children placed with foster parents
s.22 CA 1989 – General duties of local authority in relation to children looked after by it
s.61 and 62 – Duties of voluntary organisations and local authorities in relation to children accommodated by or on behalf of the voluntary organisation

Outcome

Children live in a healthy environment where their physical, emotional and psychological health is promoted and where they are able to access the services to meet their health needs.

Standard

6.1 Children's physical and emotional and social development needs are promoted.

6.2 Children understand their health needs, how to maintain a healthy lifestyle and make informed decisions about their own health.

6.3 Children are encouraged to participate in a range of positive activities that contribute to physical and emotional health.

6.4 Children have prompt access to doctors and other health professionals, including specialist services (in conjunction with the responsible authority), when they need these services.

6.5 Children's health is promoted in accordance with their placement plan and foster carers are clear about what responsibilities and decisions are delegated to them and where consent for medical treatment needs to be obtained.

6.6 Children's wishes and feelings are sought and taken into account in their health care, according to their understanding, and foster carers advocate on behalf of children.

6.7 Foster carers receive sufficient training on health and hygiene issues and first aid, with particular emphasis on health promotion and communicable diseases.

6.8 Foster carers receive guidance and training to provide appropriate care if looking after children with complex health needs.

6.9 Medicines kept in the foster home are stored safely and are accessible only by those for whom they are intended.

6.10 Foster carers are trained in the management and administration of medication. Prescribed medication is only given to the child for whom it was prescribed, and in accordance with the prescription. Children able and wishing to keep and take their own medication can do so safely.

6.11 Foster carers keep a written record of all medication, treatment and first aid given to children during placement.

6.12 Any physical adaptations or equipment needed for the appropriate care for children are provided to foster carers.

Child-Focused Standards

Standard 7 – Leisure Activities

Underpinning Legislation

Regulation 16 – Education, employment and leisure activities

Outcome

Children are able to enjoy their interests, develop confidence in their skills and are supported and encouraged to engage in leisure activities. Children are able to make a positive contribution to the foster home and their wider community.

Standard

7.1 Children develop their emotional, intellectual, social, creative and physical skills through the accessible and stimulating environment created within the foster home. Children are supported to take part in school-based and out of school activities.

7.2 Children pursue individual interests and hobbies. They take part in a range of activities, including leisure activities and trips.

7.3 Foster carers understand what is in the child's placement plan and have clarity about decisions they can make about the day to day arrangements for the child, including such matters as education, leisure activities, overnight stays, holidays, and personal issues such as haircuts.

7.4 Foster carers are supported to make reasonable and appropriate decisions within the authority delegated to them, without having to seek consent unnecessarily.

7.5 Children have permission to take part in age-appropriate peer activities as would normally be granted by a reasonable parent to their children, within the framework of the placement plan. Decision-making and any assessment of risk to the child should be undertaken on the same basis as a reasonable parent would do.

Child-Focused Standards

7.6 Children are encouraged and enabled to make and sustain friendships, which may involve friends visiting and reciprocal arrangements to visit friends' homes.

7.7 Children can stay overnight, holiday with friends and relatives of their foster carer, or go on school trips, subject to requirements of the care/placement plan if carers consider it appropriate in individual circumstances. DBS checks are not normally sought as a precondition.

Standard 8 – Promoting Educational Achievement

Underpinning Legislation

Regulation 16 – Education, employment and leisure activities
s.22(3A) CA 1989 – Duty on local authority to promote educational achievement

Outcome

The education and achievement of children is actively promoted as valuable in itself and as part of their preparation for adulthood. Children are supported to achieve their educational potential.

Standard

8.1 Children, including pre-school children and older children, have a foster home which promotes a learning environment and supports their development.

8.2 Children have access to a range of educational resources to support their learning and have opportunities beyond the school day to engage in activities which promote learning.

8.3 Children are supported to attend school or alternative provision regularly.

8.4 Children are helped by their foster carer to achieve their educational or training goals and foster carers are supported to work with a child's education provider to maximise each child's achievement and to minimise any underachievement.

8.5 The fostering service has and is fully implementing a written education policy that promotes and values children's education and is understood by foster carers.

8.6 Foster carers maintain regular contact with each child's school and other education settings, attending all parents' meetings as appropriate and advocating for the child where appropriate.

8.7 Foster carers engage and work with schools, colleges and other organisations to support children's education, including advocating to help overcome any problems the child may be experiencing in their education setting. Foster carers have up-to-date information about each child's educational progress and school attendance record.

Standard 9 – Promoting & Supporting Contact

Underpinning Legislation

Regulation 14 – Duty to promote contact

Outcome

Children have, where appropriate, constructive contact with their parents, grandparents, siblings, half-siblings, families, friends and other people who play a significant role in their lives.

Standard

9.1 Children are supported and encouraged to maintain and develop family contacts and friendships, subject to any limitations or provisions set out in their care plan and any court order.

9.2 Foster carers are given practical help to support appropriate contact, including financial help where needed, alongside support to manage any difficult emotional or other issues that the child and foster carer may have as a result of contact.

9.3 Emergency restrictions on contact are only made to protect the child from significant risk to their safety or welfare and are communicated to the responsible authority within 24 hours of being imposed.

9.4 Ongoing restriction on communication by the child is agreed by the child's responsible authority, takes the child's wishes and feelings into account and is regularly reviewed in collaboration with the responsible authority.

9.5 The fostering service feeds back to the responsible authority any significant reactions a child has to contact arrangements or visits with any person.

9.6 When deciding whether to offer a placement, the fostering service works with the responsible authority in giving consideration to how the child's contact with family and significant others will be supported, particularly where a child is placed at a distance from home.

9.7 Foster carers understand what decisions about contact are delegated to them, in line with the child's care plan, and make those decisions in the child's best interests.

The above standards are not required for short breaks. For children in short breaks, the foster carer must know how to contact parents and maintain such contact as has been agreed in the short break care plan.

Standard 10 – Providing a Suitable Physical Environment for the Foster Child

Underpinning Legislation

Regulation 27 – Assessment of prospective foster parents
Schedule 3 – Information as to prospective foster parents and other members of household and family

Outcome

Children live in foster homes that provide adequate space, to a suitable standard; the child enjoys access to a range of activities which promote her/his development.

Standard

10.1 The foster home can comfortably accommodate all who live there, including, where appropriate, any suitable aids and adaptations provided and fitted by suitably trained staff when caring for a disabled child.

10.2 The foster home is warm, adequately furnished and decorated, is maintained to a good standard of cleanliness and hygiene and is in good order throughout. Outdoor spaces which are part of the premises are safe, secure and well maintained.

10.3 Foster carers are trained in health and safety issues and have guidelines on their health and safety responsibilities. Avoidable hazards are removed as is consistent with a family home.

10.4 Foster carers understand the service's policy concerning safety for children in the foster home and in vehicles used to transport foster children. The service's policy is regularly reviewed in line with the most recent guidance from relevant bodies.

Child-Focused Standards

10.5 The foster home is inspected annually, without appointment, by the fostering service to make sure that it continues to meet the needs of foster children.

10.6 In the foster home, each child over the age of threeshould have her/his own bedroom. If this is not possible, the sharing of a bedroom is agreed by each child's responsible authority and each child has her/his own area within the bedroom. Before seeking agreement for the sharing of a bedroom, the fostering service provider takes into account any potential for bullying, any history of abuse or abusive behaviour, the wishes of the children concerned and all other pertinent facts. The decision making process and outcome of the assessment are recorded in writing where bedroom sharing is agreed.

Standard 11 – Preparation for a Placement

Underpinning Legislation

Regulation 11 – Independent fostering agencies – Duty to secure welfare
s.22 CA 1989 – General duty of local authority in relation to children looked after by it
reg.22 Care Planning, Placement and Case Review (England) Regulations 2010 – Conditions to be complied with before placing a child with a local authority foster parent

Outcome

Children are welcomed into the home in a planned and sensitive manner which makes them feel loved and valued. Children feel part of the family; they are not treated differently to the foster carer's own children living in the household; the child's needs are met and they benefit from a stable placement.

Child-Focused Standards

Standard

11.1 The service has and implements clear procedures for introducing children into the foster care placement, to the foster carer and others living in the household, which cover planned and, where permitted, emergency/immediate foster care placements. They help children understand what to expect from living in the foster home.

11.2 Children are carefully matched to a foster placement. Foster carers have full information about the child (as set out in standard 3.9).

11.3 Unless an emergency placement makes it impossible, children are given information about the foster carer before arrival, and any information (including where appropriate, photographic information) they need or reasonably request about the placement, in a format appropriate to their age and understanding. Whenever possible, children are able to visit the foster carer's home and to talk with the foster carers in private prior to a placement decision being made. Children can bring their favourite possessions into the foster carer's home.

11.4 Children are given free access to the household facilities as would be consistent with reasonable arrangements in a family home. Foster carers explain everyday household rules and expectations to children.

11.5 Where children are leaving the foster family, they are helped to understand the reasons why they are leaving. Children are supported during the transition to their new placement, to independent living or to their parental home.

11.6 Foster carers are supported to maintain links with children moving on, consistent with their care plan.

Child-Focused Standards

Standard 12 – Promoting Independence & Moves to Adulthood & Leaving Care

Underpinning Legislation

Regulation 11 – Independent fostering agencies – Duty to secure welfare
s.22 CA 1989 – General duty of local authority in relation to children looked after by it

Outcome

Children are prepared for and supported into adulthood so that they can reach their potential and achieve economic wellbeing.

Standard

12.1 Children are supported to:

   a. establish positive and appropriate social and sexual relationships
   b. develop positive self-esteem and emotional resilience
   c. prepare for the world of work and/or further or higher education
   d. prepare for moving into their own accommodation
   e. develop practical skills, including shopping, buying, cooking and keeping food, washing clothes, personal self-care, and understanding and taking responsibility for personal healthcare
   f. develop financial capability, knowledge and skills
   g. know about entitlements to financial and other support after leaving care, including benefits and support from social care services.

12.2 Foster carers contribute to the development of each child's care plan, in collaboration with the child, including the pathway plan for an 'eligible' child, and work collaboratively with the young person's social worker or personal adviser in implementing the plan.

12.3 The fostering service ensures there are comprehensive arrangements for preparing and supporting young people to make the transition to

Child-Focused Standards

independence. This includes appropriate training and support to foster carers caring for young people who are approaching adulthood. Arrangements are consistent with the young person's placement plan, care plan and pathway plan and any transition plan for children with disabilities and special educational needs.

12.4 The fostering service has a policy and practical arrangements which enable children to remain with their foster carer/s into legal adulthood, for example, so that s/he may develop appropriate life skills before being required to move to more independent accommodation. Any such decisions are agreed with foster carers at a placement meeting and are detailed in a child's placement plan.

The above standards are not required for short breaks.

STANDARDS OF FOSTERING SERVICE

Standard 13 – Recruiting and Assessing Foster Carers who can Meet the Needs of Looked After Children

Underpinning Legislation

Regulation 26 – Assessment of prospective foster parents
Regulation 27 – Approval of foster parents
Regulation 28 – Reviews and termination of approval
s.22G CA 1989 – General duty of local authority to secure sufficient accommodation for looked after children

Outcome

The fostering service recruits, assesses and supports a range of foster carers to meet the needs of children they provide care for and is proactive in assessing current and future needs of children.

Standard

13.1 The local authority fostering service implements an effective strategy to ensure sufficient foster carers to be responsive to current and predicted future demands on the service. Planning for future demands covers the need for short breaks for disabled children.

13.2 People who are interested in becoming foster carers are treated fairly, without prejudice, openly and with respect. Enquiries are dealt with courteously and efficiently by staff who have the necessary knowledge and skills. Prospective foster carers are provided with timely and relevant information following their initial enquiry and are kept informed about the progress of any subsequent application for approval.

13.3 Prospective foster carers are prepared to become foster carers in a way which addresses, and gives practical techniques to manage, the issues they are likely to encounter and identifies the competencies and strengths they have or need to develop.

Standards of Fostering Service

13.4 The assessment process is set out clearly to prospective foster carers, including the:

    a. qualities, skills or aptitudes being sought or to be achieved
    b. standards to be applied in the assessment
    c. stages and content of the selection process and where possible timescales involved
    d. information to be given to applicants.

13.5 Checks are carried out in line with reg.26 and prospective foster carers understand why identity checks, relationship status and health checks, personal references and enquiries are undertaken about them and why enhanced DBS checks and vetting and barring checks are made on themselves and adult members of their households.

13.6 Prospective foster carers are considered in terms of their capacity to look after children in a safe and responsible way that meets the child's development needs.

13.7 The written report on the person's suitability to be approved as a foster carer sets out clearly all the information that the fostering panel and decision maker needs in order to make an objective approval decision. The reports are accurate, up-to-date and include evidence-based information that distinguishes between fact, opinion and third party information. The reports are prepared, signed and dated by the social worker who assessed the prospective foster carer and countersigned and dated by the fostering team manager or a team manager of another of the provider's fostering teams.

13.8 Reviews of foster carers' approval are sufficiently thorough to allow the fostering service to properly satisfy itself about their carers' ongoing suitability to foster.

13.9 Areas of concern, or need for additional support, that are identified between reviews are addressed. Such matters identified between reviews are addressed at the time they are identified, where appropriate, rather than waiting for a review.

Standard 14 – Fostering Panels & Fostering Service's Decision-Maker

Underpinning Legislation

Regulation 23 – Constitution and membership of fostering panel
Regulation 24 – Meetings of fostering panel
Regulation 26 – Assessment of prospective foster parents
Regulation 27 – Approval of foster parents
Regulation 28 – Reviews and terminations of approval

Outcome

The fostering panel and decision-maker make timely, quality and appropriate recommendations/decisions in line with the overriding objective to promote the welfare of children in foster care.

Standard

14.1 The fostering service implements clear written policies and procedures on recruitment to, and maintenance of the central list of persons considered by it to be suitable to be members of the fostering panel (the central list), and on constitution of fostering panels.

14.2 Panel/s provide a quality assurance feedback to the fostering service provider on the quality of reports being presented to the panel.

14.3 All necessary information is provided to panel members at least five working days in advance of the panel meeting to enable full and proper consideration.

14.4 The fostering panel makes its recommendation on the suitability of a prospective carer within 8 months of receipt of the prospective foster carer's application to be assessed.

14.5 Foster carers and prospective foster carers are given the opportunity to attend and be heard at all panel meetings at which their approval is being discussed and to bring a supporter to the panel if they wish.

Standards of Fostering Service

14.6 Fostering panels have access to medical expertise and legal advice, as required.

14.7 The panel Chair ensures written minutes of panel meetings are accurate and clearly cover the key issues and views expressed by panel members and record the reasons for its recommendation.

14.8 The skills, knowledge and experience of persons on the central list are sufficient to enable the service to constitute panels equipped to make competent recommendations to the fostering service provider, taking into account the nature of the children and carers that the service caters for.

14.9 The fostering service provider's decision-maker makes a considered decision that takes account of all information available to her/him, including the recommendation of the fostering panel and, if applicable, the independent review panel, within 7 working days of receipt of the recommendation and final set of panel minutes.

14.10 The foster carer or prospective foster carer is informed orally of the decision-maker's decision within two working days and written confirmation sent within five working days.

Standard 15 – Matching the Child with a Placement that Meets their Assessed Needs

Underpinning Legislation

Regulation 17 – Support, training and information for foster parents
Regulation 9 – Care Planning, Placement and Case Review (England) Regulations 2010 – placement plan; and Regulation 14 – termination of placement by the responsible authority

Standards of Fostering Service

Outcome

The responsible authority has information and support from the fostering service which it needs to facilitate an appropriate match between the carer and child, capable of meeting the child's needs; so maximising the likelihood of a stable placement.

Standard

15.1 The fostering service only suggests foster carers to local authorities as a potential match for a child if the foster carer can reasonably be expected to meet the child's assessed needs and the impact of the placement on existing household members has been considered. Where gaps are identified, the fostering service should work with the responsible authority to ensure the placement plan sets out any additional training, resource or support required.

15.2 Prior to the placement of each child, the foster carer is provided with all the information held by the fostering service that they need to carry out her/his role effectively. The information is provided in a clear, comprehensive written form and includes the support that will be available to the foster carer. The fostering service follows up with the responsible authority any gaps in the information provided to them on the child or the child's family, which may hinder the foster carer in providing a safe caring environment that meets the child's needs and enables her/him to keep the child, other children in the fostering household and the foster carer her/himself safe.

15.3 Once placed, a child is not moved from a foster placement that is willing and able to continue caring for the child, unless that is in her/his best interests, taking the child's current wishes and feelings into account, and decided (other than in an emergency) through the child's care planning process. If a placement move occurs in an emergency, the fostering service informs the responsible authority within one working day.

Standard 16 – Statement of Purpose & Children's Guide

Underpinning Legislation

Regulation 3 – Statement of purpose & children's guide
Regulation 4 – Review of statement of purpose & children's guide

Outcome

Children, their parents, foster carers, staff and the responsible/placing authority are clear about the aims and objectives of the fostering service and what services and facilities it provides. The fostering service's operation meets the aims and objectives in the statement of purpose.

Standard

16.1 The fostering service has a clear statement of purpose which is available to, and understood by, foster carers, staff and children and is reflected in any policies, procedures and guidance. It is available to the responsible authority and any parent or person with parental responsibility.

16.2 The aims and objectives of the statement of purpose are child-focused and show how the service will meet outcomes for children.

16.3 Subject to the child's age and understanding, the fostering service ensures the child receives the children's guide at the point of placement and that the foster carer explains the contents of the children's guide in a way that is accessible.

16.4 The children's guide includes a summary of what the fostering service sets out to do for children, how they can find out their rights, how a child can contact her/his IRO, the Children's Commissioner and the Chief Inspector if they wish to raise a concern with inspectors, and how to secure access to an independent advocate.

Standards of Fostering Service

16.5 Where a child requires it, the guide is available, where appropriate, through suitable alternative methods of communication, e.g. Makaton, pictures, tape recording and translation into another language.

NB. Para. 1.13 of Volume 4 indicates that if the fostering service offers 'parent and child' arrangements, these should be included in the statement of purpose.

Standard 17 – Fitness to Provide or Manage the Administration of a Fostering Service

Underpinning Legislation

Regulation 5 – Fostering agency – Fitness of provider
Regulation 6 – Fostering agency – Appointment of manager
Regulation 7 – Fostering agency – Fitness of manager
Regulation 8 – Registered person – General requirements
Regulation 10 – Local authority fostering service – Manager

Outcome

The fostering service is provided and managed by those who are suitable to work with children and have the appropriate skills, experience and qualifications to deliver an efficient and effective service.

Standard

17.1 People involved in carrying on and managing the fostering service have:

   a. good knowledge and experience of law and practice relating to looked after children
   b. business and management skills to manage the work efficiently and effectively; and
   c. financial expertise to ensure that the fostering service is run on a sound financial basis and in a professional manner.

17.2 The registered manager (or registered person, where the registered person is an individual and there is no registered manager) has:

   a. a recognised social work qualification or a professional qualification relevant to working with children at least at level 4
   b. a qualification in management at least at level 4
   c. at least two years' experience relevant to fostering within the last five years; and
   d. at least one years' experience of supervising and managing professional staff

17.3 Appointees to the role of registered manager who do not have the management qualification (above) must enrol on a management training course within six months, and obtain a relevant management qualification within three years, of their appointment.

17.4 The responsibilities and duties of the registered manager, and to whom they are accountable, are clear and understood by them. The registered manager is notified in writing of any change in the person to whom they are accountable.

17.5 The manager exercises effective leadership of the staff and operation, such that the fostering service is organised, managed and staffed in a manner that delivers the best possible child care that meets the individual needs of each fostered child and of foster carers.

NB. With respect to standard 17.2(a) and (b), for persons undertaking a qualification after January 2011, the relevant qualification will be the level 5 Diploma in leadership for Health & Social Care and Children & Young People's Services. Managers who already hold a level 4 Leadership & Management for Care Services & Health & Social Care will not need to undertake this qualification at level 5.

Standard 18 – Financial Viability & Changes Affecting Business Continuity

Underpinning Legislation

Regulation 33 – Fostering agency ceasing to carry out fostering functions – Notifications and records

Regulation 34 – Fostering agency ceasing to carry out fostering functions – New fostering service providers

Regulation 37 – Financial position

Regulation 38 – Notice of absence

Regulation 39 – Notice of changes

Regulation 40 – Appointment of liquidators, etc

Outcome

The fostering service is essentially sound. If a service is to close or substantially change, there is proper planning to make the transition for children, foster carers and staff as smooth as possible.

Standard

18.1 A qualified accountant certifies that the independent fostering agency's annual accounts indicate the service is financially viable and likely to have sufficient funding to continue to fulfil its statement of purpose for at least the next 12 months.

18.2 The registered provider has a written development plan, reviewed annually, for the future of the service, either identifying any planned changes in the operation or resources of the service, or confirming continuation of the service's current operation and resource.

18.3 If the service, for any reason, cannot adequately and consistently maintain provision which complies with regulations or National Minimum Standards, an effective plan must be established and implemented either to rectify the situation or to close down the service.

Standards of Fostering Service

18.4 The registered provider must notify the Chief Inspector (Ofsted), the responsible authority and where different, the placing authority, if closure of the service or substantial change to the service significantly affecting the care, welfare or placement of children, is likely or actively being considered. The registered person should work with the responsible authority to ensure as smooth a transition for children and foster carers as possible.

18.5 Any person or organisation temporarily responsible for a fostering service in administration or receivership, or in the process of closure or substantial change, must operate the service in the best interests of the placed children and foster carers under the circumstances that apply, in accordance with the applicable regulations and these Standards.

Standard 19 – Suitability to Work with Children

Underpinning Legislation

Regulation 20 – Fitness of workers
Regulation 21 – Employment of staff
Regulation 22 – Records with respect to fostering services
Regulation 30 – Case records relating to foster parents and others

Outcome

There is careful selection of staff, fostering households, volunteers and the central list of persons considered suitable to be members of a fostering panel and there is monitoring of such people to help prevent unsuitable people from having the opportunity to harm children.

Standard

19.1 All people working in or for the fostering service and the central list of persons considered suitable to be members of a fostering panel are interviewed as part of the selection process and have references checked

Standards of Fostering Service

to assess suitability before taking on responsibilities. Telephone enquiries are made to each referee to verify the written references.

NB. These requirements are the responsibility of Ofsted with respect to checking suitability of those seeking to carry on or manage a fostering service.

19.2 The fostering service can demonstrate, including from written records, that it consistently follows good recruitment practice, and all applicable current statutory requirements and guidance, in foster carer selection and staff and panel member recruitment. This includes Disclosure and Barring Service (DBS) checks. All personnel responsible for recruitment and selection of staff are trained in, understand and operate these good practices.

19.3 The fostering service has a record of the recruitment and vetting checks which have been carried out for foster carers and those working (including as volunteers) for the fostering service, which includes:

 a. identity checks
 b. DBS Disclosures, including the level of the Disclosure, the unique reference number (in line with eligibility to obtain such checks)
 c. checks to confirm qualifications which are a requirement and those that are considered by the fostering service to be relevant
 d. at least two references, preferably one from a current employer, and when possible a statement from each referee as to their opinion of the person's suitability to work with children
 e. checks to confirm the right to work in the UK
 f. if the person has lived outside of the UK, further checks, as are considered appropriate, where obtaining a DBS Disclosure is not sufficient to establish suitability to work with children.

19.4 The record must show the date on which each check was completed and who carried out the check. The DBS Disclosure information must be kept in secure conditions and be destroyed by secure means as soon as it is no longer needed in line with the DBS Code of Practice. Before the Disclosure is destroyed, records need to be kept as described above.

19.5 The registered person's system for recruiting staff and others includes an effective system for reaching decisions as to who is to be appointed and the circumstances in which an application should be refused in the light of any criminal convictions or other concerns about suitability that are declared or discovered through the recruitment process.

19.6 There is a whistle-blowing policy which is made known to all staff, volunteers, foster carers and panel members. This makes it a clear duty for such people to report to an appropriate authority any circumstances within the fostering service which they consider likely to significantly harm the safety, rights or welfare of any child placed by the service.

Standard 20 – Learning & Development of Foster Carers

Underpinning Legislation

Regulation 17 – Support, training and information for foster parents
Regulation 28 – Reviews and terminations of approval

Outcome

Foster carers receive the training and development they need to carry out their role effectively. A clear framework of training and development is in place and this is used as the basis for assessing foster carers' performance and identifying their training and development needs.

Standard

20.1 All new foster carers receive an induction.

20.2 All foster carers, including all members of a household who are approved foster carers, are supported to achieve the Training, Support and Development Standards for Foster Care. Short break carers who are approved foster carers are supported to achieve the Training Support & Development Standards for Short Break Carers.

NB. Information and guidance at https://www.gov.uk/government/publications/training-support-and-development-standards-for-foster-care-evidence-workbook

20.3 Foster carers are able to evidence that the Training, Support and Development Standards have been attained within 12 months of approval (or within 18 months for family and friends foster carers). For foster carers who were approved as such before April 2008, the Standards are attained by April 2011 (or by April 2012 for family and friends foster carers). Fostering households may use the same evidence workbook.

20.4 Foster carers maintain an ongoing training and development portfolio which demonstrates how they are meeting the skills required of them by the fostering service.

20.5 Foster carers' personal development plans set out how they will be supported to undertake ongoing training and development that is appropriate to their development needs and experience.

20.6 Each carer's annual review includes an appraisal of performance against clear and consistent standards set by the agency, and consideration of training and development needs, which are documented in the review report. The foster carer's personal development plan is reviewed and the effectiveness of training and development received is evaluated. The review takes into account the views of each child currently placed with the foster carer.

20.7 The fostering service is clear and transparent with their foster carers about the level of support available to them and how to access such support.

20.8 Support and training is made available to foster carers, including hard to reach carers, to assist them in meeting the specific needs of the children they are caring for or are expected to care for.

20.9 Appropriate training on safer caring is provided for all members of the foster household, including young people of sufficient age and understanding, and ensures that foster carers understand how safer

Standards of Fostering Service

caring principles should be applied in a way which meets the needs of individual children.

20.10 All training fits within a framework of equal opportunities and anti-discriminatory practice and is organised to encourage and facilitate attendance by foster carers.

20.11 In cases where a foster carer moves to a new fostering service, details of the development and training which he or she has undertaken – and of the extent to which the agreed training and development standards have been met – are made available on request to the new provider and the foster carer is able to take their training and development portfolio with them.

Standard 21 – Supervision & Support of Foster Carers

Underpinning Legislation

Regulation 17 – Support, training and information for foster parents

Outcome

Foster carers receive the support and supervision they need in order to care properly for children placed with them.

Standard

21.1 The fostering service supports its foster carers to ensure it provides foster children with care that reasonably meets those children's needs, takes the children's wishes and feelings into account, actively promotes individual care and supports the children's safety, health, enjoyment, education and preparation for the future.

21.2 The fostering service ensures foster carers understand the nature and level of support which will be provided to them by the fostering service.

Standards of Fostering Service

21.3 There is an effective out of hours advice and support service for foster carers.

21.4 Peer support, foster care associations and/or self-help groups for foster carers are encouraged and supported.

21.5 Foster carers are provided with breaks from caring, for example, short breaks, if appropriate. These are planned to take account of the needs of any children placed.

21.6 All foster carers have access to adequate social work and other professional support, information and advice, to enable them to provide consistent, high quality care to the child. This includes assistance with dealing with relevant services, such as health and education. Consideration is given to any help or support needed by the sons and daughters of foster carers.

21.7 The role of the supervising social worker is clear both to the worker and the foster carer.

21.8 Each approved foster carer is supervised by a named, appropriately qualified social worker who has meetings with the foster carer, including at least one unannounced visit a year. Meetings have a clear purpose and provide the opportunity to supervise the foster carer's work, ensure the foster carer is meeting the child's needs, taking into account the child's wishes and feelings, and offer support and a framework to assess the carer's performance and develop their competencies and skills. The frequency of meetings for short break foster carers should be proportionate to the amount of care provided. Foster carers' files include records of supervisory meetings.

21.9 The supervising social worker ensures each foster carer s/he supervises is informed in writing of, and accepts, understands and operates within, all regulations and standards and with policies and guidance agreed by the fostering service.

21.10 On approval, foster carers are given information, either a handbook or electronic resources, which cover policies, procedures (including with regard to allegations), guidance, financial information, legal information and insurance details. This information is updated regularly.

Standards of Fostering Service

21.11 Current and prospective foster carers are able to make a complaint about any aspect of the service which affects them directly. Records are kept of complaints and representations, how they are dealt with, the outcome and any action taken. These records are reviewed regularly so that the service's practice is improved where necessary.

21.12 There is a good system of communication between the fostering service social workers and the child's social worker. The fostering service social workers understand the role of the child's social worker and work effectively with them.

Standard 22 – Handling Allegations & Suspicions of Harm

Underpinning Legislation

Regulation 11 – Independent fostering agencies – Duty to secure welfare
Regulation 12 – Arrangements for the protection of children
Regulation 17 – Support, training and information for foster parents
Regulation 30 – Case records relating to foster carers and others
Regulation 36 – Notifiable events
s.22 CA 1989 – General duties of local authority in relation to children placed by it
s.61 and 62 – Duties of voluntary organisations and local authorities in relation to children accommodated by or on behalf of the voluntary organisation

Outcome

Allegations and suspicions of harm are handled in a way that provides effective protection and support for children, the person making the allegation, and at the same time supports the person who is the subject of the allegation.

Standards of Fostering Service

Standard

22.1 All foster carers, fostering service staff and volunteers understand what they must do if they receive an allegation or have suspicions that a person may have:

   a. behaved in a way that has, or may have, harmed a child
   b. possibly committed a criminal offence against or related to a child or
   c. behaved towards a child in a way that indicates s/he is unsuitable to work with children

   The fostering service ensures required actions are taken, or have been taken, in any relevant situation of which it is aware.

22.2 The fostering services procedure is in line with Government guidance and requirements, including the duty to refer information to statutory bodies. It is known to foster carers, fostering service staff, volunteers and children.

   NB. See https://www.gov.uk/disclosure-barring-service-check/dbs-barred-lists

22.3 A copy of the fostering service provider's child protection procedures is made available to foster carers, fostering service staff, volunteers and children. Any comments on these are taken into account by the provider.

22.4 The fostering service provider's child protection procedures are submitted for consideration and comment to the Local Safeguarding Children Board (LSCB) and Local Authority Designated Officer (LADO) for child protection (or other senior officer responsible for child protection matters). They are consistent with the local policies and procedures agreed by the LSCB relevant to the geographical area where the foster carer lives. Any conflicts between locally agreed procedures and those of other placing authorities are discussed and resolved as far as possible.

22.5 Each fostering service has a designated person, who is a senior manager, responsible for managing allegations. The designated person has responsibility for liaising with the local authority designated officer

Standards of Fostering Service

(LADO) and for keeping the subject of the allegation informed of progress during and after the investigation.

22.6 Allegations against people working with children or members of the fostering household are reported by the fostering service to the LADO, including allegations that on the face of it may appear relatively insignificant or have been reported directly to police or Children and Family Services.

22.7 A clear and comprehensive summary of any allegations made against a particular member of the fostering household, or staff member, including details of how the allegation was followed up and resolved, a record of any action taken and the decisions reached, is kept on the person's confidential file. A copy is provided to the person as soon as the investigation is concluded. The information is retained on the confidential file, even after someone leaves the organisation, until the person reaches normal retirement age, or for 10 years if this is longer.

22.8 As soon as possible after an investigation into a foster carer is concluded, her/his approval as suitable to foster is reviewed. There is a clear policy framework which outlines the circumstances in which a foster carer should be removed as one of the fostering service provider's approved foster carers, in the interests of the safety or welfare of children. This is available to foster carers.

22.9 Investigations into allegations or suspicions of harm are handled fairly, quickly, and consistently in a way that provides effective protection for the child, and at the same time supports the person who is the subject of the allegation. Fostering services follow the framework for managing cases of allegations of abuse against people who work with children as set out in *Working Together to Safeguard Children 2013*.

22.10 Fostering services ensure a clear distinction is made between investigation into allegations of harm and discussions over standards of care. Investigations which find no evidence of harm should not become procedures looking into poor standards of care – these should be treated separately.

Standards of Fostering Service

22.11 There is written guidance for foster carers and staff, which makes clear how they will be supported during an investigation into an allegation including payment of allowance and any fee to foster carers while investigations are ongoing.

22.12 During an investigation the fostering service makes support, which is independent of the fostering service, available to the person subject to the allegation and, where this is a foster carer, to their household, in order to provide:

   a. information and advice about the process
   b. emotional support; and
   c. if needed, mediation between the foster carer and the fostering service and/or advocacy (including attendance at meetings and panel hearings).

NB. Volume 4 paras. 3.68–3.81 offer further guidance about how allegations should be managed in terms of support of carers, the need for a designated person in each fostering service and a distinction between allegations of harm and discussions over standards of care, payment of fees during an investigation and required timescales.

Standard 23 – Learning, Development & Qualification of Staff

Underpinning Legislation

Regulation 19 – Staffing of fostering service

Outcome

Children and foster carers receive a service from staff, volunteers and panel members and decision-makers who have the competence to meet their needs.

Standards of Fostering Service

Standard

23.1 There is a good quality learning and development programme, which includes induction, post-qualifying and in-service training, that staff and volunteers are supported to undertake. The programme equips them with the skills required to meet the needs of the children, keeps them up-to-date with professional, legal and practice developments and reflects the policies, legal obligations and business needs of the fostering service.

23.2 The learning and development programme is evaluated for effectiveness at least annually and is updated where necessary.

23.3 New staff and volunteers undertake the Children's Workforce Development Council's induction standards, commencing within 7 working days of starting employment and completed in six months.

N.B. CWDC has been disbanded.

23.4 All social workers and other specialists (e.g. medical, legal, educationalists, psychologists, therapists) are professionally qualified and, where applicable, registered by the appropriate professional body. They are appropriately trained to work with children, their families and foster carers, and have a good understanding of foster care and the policies and purpose of the fostering service.

23.5 Assessment and appraisal of all staff involved in fostering work takes account of identified skills needed for particular roles and is used to identify individuals' learning and development needs.

23.6 Any staff involved in assessing the suitability of persons to be foster carers are social workers, have experience of foster care and family placement work and are trained in assessment. Social work students and social workers who do not have the relevant experience only carry out assessments under the supervision of an appropriately experienced social worker, who takes responsibility for the assessment.

23.7 When unqualified staff and volunteers carry out social work functions, they do so under the direct supervision of experienced social workers, who are accountable for their work.

Standards of Fostering Service

23.8 Persons joining the central list of persons considered to be suitable to be fostering panel members are provided with an opportunity to observe a fostering panel meeting.

23.9 Each person on the central list is given induction training which is completed within 10 weeks of becoming a panel member.

23.10 Each person on the central list is given the opportunity of attending an annual joint training day with the agency's fostering staff.

23.11 Each panel member has access to appropriate training and skills development and is kept abreast of relevant changes to legislation, regulation and guidance.

23.12 The fostering service's decision-maker is a senior person within the fostering service, or is a trustee or director of the fostering service, who is a social worker with at least three years' post-qualifying experience in childcare social work and has knowledge and experience of permanency planning for children and childcare law and practice.

Standard 24 – Staff Support & Supervision

Underpinning Legislation

Regulation 19 – Staffing of fostering service
Regulation 20 – Fitness of workers

Outcome

Staff and volunteers are supported and guided to fulfill their roles and provide a high quality service to children.

Standard

24.1 The employer is fair and competent, with sound employment practices and good support for all its staff and volunteers.

Standards of Fostering Service

24.2 All staff, volunteers and the registered person are properly managed, supported and understand to whom they are accountable.

24.3 Suitable arrangements exist for professional supervision of the registered person of the agency.

24.4 Staff have access to support and advice, and are provided with regular supervision by appropriately qualified and experienced staff.

24.5 A written record is kept by the agency detailing the time, date and length of each supervision held for each member of staff, including the registered person. The record is signed by the supervisor and the member of staff at the end of the supervision.

24.6 All staff have their performance individually and formally appraised at least annually and, where they are working with children, this appraisal takes into account any views of children the service is providing for.

24.7 Staff and volunteers are able to access the specialist advice needed to provide a comprehensive service for children, including legal advice.

Standard 25 – Managing Effectively & Efficiently & Monitoring the Service

Underpinning Legislation

Regulation 8 – Fostering agency registered person – General requirements
Regulation 10 – Local authority fostering service – Manager
Regulation 18 – Independent fostering agencies – Representations and complaints
Regulation 35 – Review of quality of care
Regulation 36 – Notifiable events
Regulation 37 – Financial position

Standards of Fostering Service

Outcome

The fostering service is managed ethically, effectively and efficiently, delivering a service which meets the needs of its users.

Standard

25.1 There are clear and effective procedures for monitoring and controlling the activities of the service. This includes the financial viability of the service, any serious incidents, allegations or complaints about the service and ensuring the quality of the service.

25.2 The manager regularly monitors all records kept by the service to ensure compliance with the service's policies, to identify any concerns about specific incidents and to identify patterns and trends. Immediate action is taken to address any issues raised by this monitoring.

25.3 Management of the service ensures all staff's work and all fostering activity is consistent with these regulations and National Minimum Standards and with the service's policies and procedures.

25.4 Managers, staff, volunteers and foster carers are clear about their roles and responsibilities. The level of delegation and responsibility of the manager, and the lines of accountability, are clearly defined.

25.5 Clear arrangements are in place to identify the person in charge when the registered manager is absent.

25.6 The registered person ensures copies of inspection reports by Ofsted are made available to all members of staff, to their foster carers, children fostered by the service and their parents/carers, and, on request, to the responsible or, where different, placing authorities of existing foster children or those considering placing a child through the service.

25.7 The executive side of the local authority or the independent foster service's provider/trustees, board members or management committee members:

   a. receive written reports on the management, outcomes and financial state of the fostering service every three months

Standards of Fostering Service

    b. monitor the management and outcomes of the services in order to satisfy themselves that the service is effective and is achieving good outcomes for children

    c. satisfy themselves that the provider is complying with the conditions of registration.

25.8 The registered person takes action to address any issue of concern s/he identifies or which is raised with her/him.

25.9 Staff, volunteers and foster carers have a copy of:

    a. policies and working practices in respect of grievances and disciplinary matters

    b. details of the services offered

    c. the equal opportunities policy

    d. health and safety procedures

25.10 Information is provided to commissioners of services as part of tendering. This includes:

    a. charges for each of its services

    b. statements of the amounts paid to foster carers (separated by fee and allowance) and

    c. amounts paid for other services e.g. health/education.

25.11 The registered person has provided the service with a written policy and procedural guidelines on considering and responding to representations and complaints in accordance with legal requirements and relevant statutory guidance.

25.12 The service has the facilities to work with children with physical, sensory and learning impairments, communication difficulties or for whom English is not their first language. Oral and written communications are made available in a format appropriate to the physical, sensory and learning impairments; communication difficulties and language of the individual. Procedures include arrangements for reading, translating, Makaton, pictures, tape recording and explaining documents to those unable to understand the document.

Standards of Fostering Service

Standard 26 – Records

Underpinning Legislation

Regulation 22 – Records with respect to the fostering services
Regulation 26 – Assessment of prospective foster parents
Regulation 30 – Case records relating to foster carers and others
Regulation 31 – Register of foster carers
Regulation 32 – Retention and confidentiality of records
Regulation 33 – Fostering agency ceasing to carry out fostering functions – Notifications and records

Outcome

Records are clear, up to date and stored securely, and contribute to an understanding of the child's life.

Standard

26.1 The fostering service has and implements a written policy that clarifies the purpose, format and content of information to be kept on the fostering service's files, on the child's files and on case files relating to foster carers.

26.2 Staff, volunteers, panel members and fostering households understand the nature of records maintained and follow the service's policy for the keeping and retention of files, managing confidential information and access to files (including files removed from the premises). There is a system in place to monitor the quality and adequacy of record keeping and take action when needed.

26.3 Children and their parents understand the nature of records maintained and how to access them.

26.4 Information about individual children is kept confidential and only shared with those who have a legitimate and current need to know the information, and to those parts of a child's record or other information that they need to know.

Standards of Fostering Service

26.5 Entries in records, decisions and reasons, are legible, clearly expressed, non-stigmatising and distinguish between fact, opinion and third party information, and are signed and dated.

26.6 Information about the child is recorded clearly and in a way which will be helpful to the child when they access their files now or in the future. Children are actively encouraged to read their files, other than necessarily confidential or third party information, and to correct errors and add personal statements.

26.7 The foster carer understands the important supporting role they play in encouraging the child to reflect on and understand their history. The child, subject to age and understanding, is encouraged to keep appropriate memorabilia (including photographs) of her/his time in the placement. The fostering service makes this role clear to their foster carers and ensures they can record, and help children make a record of (subject to age and understanding), significant life events.

26.8 When there is an agency placement, the agency works with the responsible authority to ensure effective integration of information held in the agency's case files and those of the responsible authority. On receipt of a written request by a child's responsible authority, the agency immediately provides copies of records and documents in relation to the child.

26.9 When a foster carer seeks to move to a new provider, the new provider seeks information from the previous provider about the prospective foster carer, and the previous provider complies with such a request within one month of receipt of the written request.

Standard 27 – Fitness of Premises for use as a Fostering Service

Underpinning Legislation

Regulation 32 – Retention and confidentiality of records

Standards of Fostering Service

Outcome

The premises and administrative systems are suitable to enable the service to meet the objectives of its statement of purpose.

Standard

27.1 There are efficient and robust administrative systems, including IT and communication systems. Premises have:

   a. facilities for the secure retention of records
   b. appropriate measures to safeguard IT systems and
   c. an appropriate security system

27.2 The premises and its contents are insured (or there are alternative prompt methods of replacing lost items).

27.3 The provider has a business continuity plan, which staff understand and can access, which will include both provision of premises and safeguarding/back up of records.

Standard 28 – Payment to Carers

Underpinning Legislation

Regulation 17 – Support, information and training for foster parents
Regulation 27 – Approval of foster parents
Sch.5 – Matters and obligations in foster care agreements

Outcome

Payments to foster carers are fair and paid in a timely way. Foster carers are clear about the fostering service's payment structure and payments due to them.

Standards of Fostering Service

Standard

28.1 Each foster carer receives at least the national minimum allowance for the child, plus any necessary agreed expenses for the care, education and reasonable leisure interests of the child or young person, including insurance, holidays, birthdays, school trips, religious festivals, etc, which cover the full cost of caring for each child placed with her/him.

28.2 Payments of allowances and any fees paid are made promptly at the agreed time and foster carers are provided with a statement of payment at the end of each tax year.

28.3 Allowances and any fees paid are reviewed annually and the fostering service consults with foster carers in advance to changes to the allowance and fees.

28.4 The fostering service advises foster carers of financial and other support that is available to foster carers where a child remains with them after they reach the age of 18 or where they care for a parent/s and child.

28.5 There is a clear and transparent written policy on payments to foster carers that sets out the criteria for calculating payments and distinguishes between the allowance paid and any fee paid. The policy includes policy on payment of allowances and any fee during a break in placement or should the fostering household be subject to an allegation.

28.6 The written policy and the current level of payments are provided annually to each foster carer and commissioners of the service. The foster carer receives clear information about the allowances and expenses payable and how to access them, before a child is placed.

28.7 Criteria for calculating fees and allowances are applied equally to all foster carers, whether the foster carer is related to the child or unrelated, or the placement is short or long term.

28.8 Fostering service providers are clear about what equipment is being either loaned or given to foster carers.

28.9 When a child is eligible for benefits as a result of a disability, foster carers are encouraged to apply for those benefits. There are regular recorded discussions about how any additional benefits are being spent to promote the best interests of the child.

Standard 29 – Notification of Significant Events

Underpinning Legislation

Regulation 36 – Notifiable events
Sch.7 – Events and notifications

Outcome

All significant events relating to the protection of children by the service are notified by the registered person to the appropriate authorities.

Standard

29.1 The registered person has a system in place to notify, within 24 hours, persons and appropriate authorities of the occurrence of significant events in accordance with reg.36. The system includes what to do if a notifiable event arises at the weekend.

29.2 A written record is kept which includes details of the action taken, and the outcome of any action or investigation, following a notifiable event.

29.3 The registered person has a system for notification to responsible authorities of any serious concerns about the emotional or mental health of a child, such that a mental health assessment would be requested under the Mental Health Act 1983.

29.4 Following an incident notifiable under reg.36, the registered person contacts the responsible authority to discuss any further action that may need to be taken.

Standard 30 – Family & Friends as Foster Carers

Underpinning Legislation

Regulation 17 – Support, training and information for foster parents
Regulations 24 and 25 Care Planning, Placement and Case Review (England) Regulations 2010.

Outcome

Family and friends foster carers receive the support they require to meet the needs of children placed with them.

Standard

30.1 The needs and circumstances of family and friends foster carers are taken into account when determining the fostering service's policies and practices.

30.2 The fostering service's statement of purpose includes the services and facilities that it provides to family and friends foster carers.

30.3 In deciding whether a relative, friend or other connected person should be approved as a foster carer, the decision-maker takes into account the needs, wishes and feelings of the child and the capacity of the carer to meet these.

30.4 In seeking to support family and friends foster carers, the local authority fostering service works closely with the wider local authority children's services department, other departments, and agencies such as housing, to mitigate any limitations to the carer's capacity to care for a foster child.

30.5 When assessing an individual's suitability to be a family and friends foster carer, the likely length of the placement, the age of the child, the wishes and feelings and any concerns of the child and, if appropriate, the capacity of the wider family to contribute to the child's long term care are taken into account.

Standards of Fostering Service

30.6 Potential family and friends foster carers should be provided with information about the assessment process, so they know what is expected of them, how they will be assessed, including the criteria that will be used and how particular issues for family and friends foster carers will be addressed, and any support offered during the assessment process.

30.7 Family and friends foster carers are asked about their existing knowledge of the foster child's behaviour and background and any concerns they have about the child, as well as being provided with information about the child that is held by the fostering service.

30.8 The child's introduction to the new fostering arrangement takes account of the fact that, whilst the child may know the carer well, the carer's role in the child's life is now changing. This is explained to the child and the carer is provided with the support they need to manage this transition.

30.9 The fostering service takes into account the carer's, parents' and child's views about contact before the start of the placement, or as soon as possible afterwards, and puts in place appropriate supports to help manage contact.

30.10 Financial and other support is provided to all foster carers according to objective criteria that do not discriminate against foster carers that have a pre-existing relationship with the child. Family and friends foster carers may require some services to be delivered in a different way, but there should be equity of provision and entitlement.

30.11 Family and friends foster carers have access to training available to other foster carers, but the fostering service provider also offers training that addresses the particular needs and circumstances of family and friends foster carers.

30.12 Family and friends foster carers have access to support groups that meet their particular needs.

30.13 Supervising social workers who are supporting family and friends foster carers have training in the particular needs and circumstances of this group.

30.14 When a family and friends foster carer is temporarily approved as a foster carer under reg.24 of the Care Planning, Placement and Case Review (England) Regulations 2010, a full assessment is competed as soon as practicable, where the intention is for the child to stay with the carer, and always within the statutory timeframe set out in the regulations.

NB. This standard only applies to local authority fostering services and those independent fostering services which approve family and friends foster carers. However, if family and friends are approved as foster carers, the other standards apply as they do for other carers.

Standard 31 – Placement Plan & Review

Underpinning Legislation

Sch.5 – Matters and obligations in foster care agreements
Care Planning, Placement & Review (England) Regulations 2010; Regulation 9 – Placement plan, & Part 6 – Reviews of the child's case

Outcome

Children are cared for in line with their placement plan/short break care plan. The fostering service takes action to chase up outstanding reviews or visits from the responsible authority, contributes to those reviews and assists the child to contribute to their reviews.

Standard

- 31.1. The fostering service supports foster carers to play an active role in agreeing the contents of each child's placement plan in conjunction with the responsible authority.

- 31.2 The foster carer is given a copy of the child's placement plan as soon as this is provided to the agency by the responsible authority. If provision

Standards of Fostering Service

of the care plan by the responsible authority is delayed, the fostering service provider follows this up with the responsible authority.

31.3 The foster carer is supported to contribute effectively to the review of the care plan which includes the placement plan.

31.4 The foster carer is supported to assist the child to put forward her/his views, wishes and feelings as part of each review process, and the fostering service helps to ensure that these are fully taken into account by the child's responsible authority.

31.5 Foster carers are supported to explain the child's care plan and any changes to those plans, to the child.

31.6 The fostering service contacts the responsible authority to request statutory reviews or visits if these are overdue for any child or if a review has not already been arranged by the responsible authority and a change in the care plan is needed; there has been a significant change in arrangements for the child's care or a major action (e.g. a change of placement) which is not in the care plan appears likely.

31.7 The fostering service provider and foster carer contribute effectively to each child's placement plan review and statutory review of the child's care plan.

31.8 Children are assisted to secure an independent advocate to support them in providing their views, wishes and feelings to statutory views.

FEES & FREQUENCY OF INSPECTIONS

Registration Fees [The Her Majesty's Chief Inspector of Education, Children's Services & Skills (Fees & Frequency of Inspections) (Children's Homes etc) Regulations 2015]

Application for Registration [Reg.8]

- The fee to accompany an application for registration by a person seeking to be registered as a person who carries on a fostering agency: £2,646.00

- Application for registration by a person seeking to be registered as a person who manages a fostering agency: £910.00 [reg.8].

Variation Fees [reg.16]

- Application under s.15(1)(a) CSA 2000 – (variation or removal of any condition for time being in force in relation to the registration): £1,322.00

- The fee for 'minor variation' (i.e. if successful, not requiring a material alteration to the register maintained by Ofsted under s.11(4) CSA 2000) is: £160.00

Annual Fee

- For a local authority: £3,216.00 [reg.26]

- For an independent fostering agency: £2,830.00 [reg.22]

    NB. The above fees were correct as at April 2020 and are likely to rise over time.

Inspections [reg.19]

- The Chief Inspector must arrange for premises that are used for the purposes of a fostering agency or a local authority fostering service to be inspected at least once every three years.

- Any such inspection may be unannounced.

Appendix 1: Source Documents

- CA 1989
- Care Standards Act 2000
- Children and Families Act 2014
- Care Planning, Placement & Case Review (England) Regulations 2010
- Care Planning, Placement and Case Review and Fostering Services (Miscellaneous Amendments) Regulations 2013
- Children's Homes and Looked After Children ((Miscellaneous Amendments) (England) Regulations 2013
- Care Planning and Fostering (Miscellaneous Amendments) (England) Regulations 2015
- Fostering Services (England) Regulations 2011
- The Care Planning, Placement and Case Review and Fostering Services (Miscellaneous Amendments) Regulations 2013
- Her Majesty's Chief Inspector of Education, Children's Services and Skills (Fees and Frequency of Inspections) (Children's Homes etc.) 2015
- The Independent Review of Determinations (Adoption and Fostering) Regulations 2009
- National Minimum Fostering Standards (2011)
- CA 1989 Guidance and Regulations (as amended) Vols. 1–5 (delegation of authority to carers; assessment and approval of potential carers; family and friends placements; contact with siblings; information sharing)
- Working Together to Safeguard Children 2018
- Getting the Best from Complaints; Social Care Complaints and Representations for Children, Young People and Others, DCSF 2006

Appendix 1: Source Documents

- Statutory guidance: Promoting the Health and Wellbeing of Looked After Children, DfE March 2015
- Statutory guidance: Promoting the Education of Looked After and Previously Looked After Children, DfE February 2018
- Statutory guidance: Securing Sufficient Accommodation for Looked After Children, DCSF 2010
- Statutory guidance: How to Safeguard and Promote the Welfare of Disabled Children using Short Breaks, DCSF 2010
- Statutory guidance: Independent Reviewing Officers and Local Authorities on their Functions in Relation to Case Management and Review for Looked After Children, DCSF 2010
- Statutory guidance: Care of Unaccompanied Migrant Children and Child Victims of Modern Slavery, November 2017
- Statutory guidance: Designated Teachers for Looked After and Previously Looked After Children, February 2018
- Statutory guidance: Staying Put – Arrangements for Care Leavers Aged 18 and Above to Stay On with their Former Foster Carers, May 2013
- Statutory guidance: Children who Run Away or Go Missing from Home or Care, DfE January 2014
- Care for Unaccompanied and Trafficked Children January, 2014
- Keeping Children Safe in Education: Statutory guidance for schools and colleges, DfE September 2019
- Junior Individual Saving Accounts and Child Trust Funds for Looked After Children: (was due for review by January 2019)

Appendix 2: Foster Carers' Charter

- This charter was published by the Secretary of State for Children's Services in April 2011, having been developed by the government in consultation with the British Association for Adoption and Fostering, the Fostering Network and the Association of Directors of Children's Services.
- Children come first:
  - Children in foster care deserve to experience as full a family life as possible, as part of a loving foster family with carers who can make everyday decisions as they would their own child and without the child feeling that they "stand out" as a looked after child
  - Children must be given every support to develop their own identities and aspirations, fulfil their potential, and take advantage of all opportunities to promote their talents and skills. Above all, they should be listened to.
- Local authorities and fostering services must:
  - Recognise in practice the importance of the child's relationship with his or her foster family as one that can make the biggest difference in the child's life and which can endure into adulthood
  - Listen to, involve foster carers and their foster children in decision-making and planning, and provide foster carers and their foster children with full information about each other
  - In making placements, be clear about the continuing care or support there will be (including for the child into adulthood), sensitive to the needs of the foster carer and the child in making and ending placements, and have contingency plans should the placement not work
  - Treat foster carers with openness, fairness and respect as a core member of the team around the child and support them in making reasonable and appropriate decisions on behalf of their foster child
  - Ensure that foster carers have the support services and development opportunities they need in order to provide their foster child with the

Appendix 2: Foster Carers' Charter

> best possible care. That includes liaising with local foster carers groups and seeking to respond to problems and disseminate best practice
> - Make sure foster carers are recompensed on time and are given clear information about any support, allowances, fees, and holidays they will receive including in cases of dispute with the service or during gaps in placements.

- Foster carers must:
  - Provide positive adult role models, treat the foster child as they would their own child, and be a "pushy parent" in advocating for all aspects of the child's development, including educational attainment and physical and emotional health and wellbeing and co-operate fully as part of a team with other key professionals in the child's life
  - Support their foster child and do all they can to make the placement work. Take part in learning and development, use skills and approaches that make a positive impact and enable the child to reach his or her potential. Support their foster child to help them to counter possible bullying and discrimination as a result of their care status.

Further Reading

Useful books from CoramBAAF

- *Adoption Now: Law, regulations, guidance and standards*, Fergus Smith and Roy Stewart with Alexandra Conroy Harris, 2013
  A handy guide to adoption law in England and Wales.

- *Adoption and Children (Scotland) Act 2007: The Act and Regulations*, Fergus Smith and Roy Stewart with Alistair Stobie, 2011
  A handy guide to the Adoption and Children (Scotland) Act 2007.

- *Key Changes to Family Justice*, Shefali Shah, 2016
  A guide exploring recent legislative changes in England, including the Family Justice Review, Children and Families Act 2014 and the impact of *Re B* and *Re B-S*.

- *Child Care Law: A summary of the law in England and Wales*, Deborah Cullen and Alexandra Conroy Harris, 2019
  A guide to law pertaining to child care in England and Wales.

- *Child Care Law: A summary of the law in Scotland*, Alexandra Plumtree, 2014
  A guide to law pertaining to child care in Scotland.

- *Child Care Law: A summary of the law in Northern Ireland*, Michael Long, 2018
  A guide to law pertaining to child care in Northern Ireland.

- *Thinking about Fostering?*, Henrietta Bond, 2016
  A unique introductory guide to foster care for those thinking about fostering a child.

- *Fostering: What it is and what it means*, Shaila Shah, 2016
  A short, brightly illustrated children's guide to fostering, covering all the commonly asked questions.

- *Effective Fostering Panels*, Sarah Borthwick and Jenifer Lord, 2019

Further Reading

This bestselling guide offers good practice points to agencies in the operation of effective fostering panels.

- *We are Fostering*, Jean Camis, 2003
  A colourful workbook for birth children in foster families, including space for drawings and photographs.

- *Ten Tip Tips on Going to Court*, Alexandra Conroy Harris, 2014
  A concise, practical guide looking at steps that workers can take to prepare for and get the most out of going to court – before, during and after the hearing.

- *What Happens in Court?*, Hedi Argent and Mary Lane, 2003
  A user-friendly children's guide to help children understand the role a court might have in their lives.

All available from CoramBAAF, 41 Brunswick Square, London WC1N 1AZ. Visit www.corambaaf.org.uk/bookshop or contact Publications Sales on 020 7520 7515.